TEACHING WITHOUT BELLS

What We Can Learn from Powerful

Practice in Small Schools

Joey Feldman

TEACHER'S TOOLKIT SERIES

Paradigm Publishers
Boulder • London

Copyright © 2010 Paradigm Publishers

Published in the United States by Paradigm Publishers, 2845 Wilderness Place, Suite 200, Boulder, CO 80301 USA.

Paradigm Publishers is the trade name of Birkenkamp & Company, LLC, Dean Birkenkamp, President and Publisher.

Library of Congress Cataloging-in-Publication Data for this book is available from the Library of Congress

ISBN 978-1-59451-841-6 (paperback : alk. paper)

Printed and bound in the United States of America on acid-free paper that meets the standards of the American National Standard for Permanence of Paper for Printed Library Materials.

Design by Cindy Young.

14 13 12 11 10   1 2 3 4 5

TEACHING WITHOUT BELLS

TEACHER'S TOOLKIT SERIES

CONTENTS

SERIES FOREWORD

THIS TEACHER'S TOOLKIT series is a set of six related books written for prospective, new, and experienced teachers who are committed to students and families, who conceive of themselves as agents of democratic change, and who are eager to think more deeply, more broadly, and more practically about their work in education. All six books succinctly link theory with practice, present extended arguments for improving education, and wrap their discussions around successful examples of the topics in question.

Although each book is its own resource, the books in the Toolkit series share some common views about teaching. For one, all of the books treat teachers not as mere deliverers of curriculum but as active, three-dimensional professionals capable of diagnosing student learning, developing powerful educational experiences, assessing and adjusting student learning, and forming productive relationships with children and adults in schools. Another view all of the books share is that teaching is hard work that is among the most important kinds of work any society requires. My grandmother used to say that no society can survive without farmers or teachers. I think that is still true. Teaching is undeniably difficult work, but it is also frequently enjoyable work because it is so challenging, meaningful, and success oriented. These books are for teachers who have accepted the challenges of teaching because they relish the satisfaction of the work, they enjoy helping young people grow, and they know that quality education is necessary for the health of our world.

A third commonality about teaching among these books is their shared presumption that teachers are always looking for ways to improve. Teaching is a profession in which one enters as a novice, develops expertise over time, and continues to grow and change throughout the whole of one's career. The Toolkit books are written for teachers at multiple points in their career cycle: Beginning teachers will learn new ways to think about learning, students, and about what it means to become a successful educator. Early- and middle-career teachers can reflect on their own practice in light of the ideas, strategies, and stories of these books—and they can use the books to deepen and broaden their future work. Veteran teachers can see themselves and their varied experiences inside the perspectives of the books, as well as figure out how they can continue to challenge themselves and their students—and perhaps take on other kinds of education work such as mentoring newer teachers, advocating for students on a broader stage, or writing about their own teaching. No matter where readers are in their education careers, these books offer powerful learning and useful opportunities for professional reflection.

The six books are sequenced to loosely follow both the career cycle of teaching and the fact that, as teachers progress, they often widen their sphere of influence. Book 1 in the series is *Teaching for Success: Developing Your Teacher Identity in Today's Classroom*, by Brad Olsen. This book focuses on the processes of "becoming a teacher" and explores how to teach well in this contemporary age. Wrapping its conversations about teacher development around the core concept of teacher identity, the book offers its own teacher learning experience: how to recognize, adjust, and maximize the many ways your personal self and your professional self become integrated in your teaching work.

Book 2, *Teaching English Learners: Fostering Language and the Democratic Experience*, by Kip Téllez, focuses on what teachers can do in their classrooms in order to better understand and more effectively teach English learners. Drawing from research and experience not only on learning and teaching but also on culture, language, immigration, and contemporary politics, Téllez offers a unique guide for use by U.S. teachers interested in deeply and compassionately supporting the growth of students whose native language is not English.

Book 3 in the series is *Teaching Without Bells: What We Can Learn from Powerful Instruction in Small Schools*, by Joey Feldman. This book offers a valuable look at how teaching and learning are fundamentally influenced by school size. The book's premise is that student and teacher experiences in education are direct functions of their school's size (and its accompanying influence on how schools are organized). Focusing on challenges and benefits of teaching in small high schools, Feldman's book helps readers consider where they might want to teach and—no matter the size of their school site—how they can teach well by maximizing lessons from the small schools movement.

Book 4, *Leading from the Inside Out: Expanded Roles for Teachers in Equitable Schools*, by Norton Grubb and Lynda Tredway, opens up the professional world of the teacher by offering new ways to think about school reform from the vantage point of the teacher. The authors make a compelling case for teachers as the key ingredient in education reform and schools as the lever for democratic educational change. Presenting a blueprint for a new kind of school in which teachers are not only classroom instructors but education reformers as well, Grubb and Tredway illustrate why we have the schools we have today and how broad-minded teachers can transform them into successful schools for tomorrow.

Book 5, *Teaching Toward Democracy: Educators as Agents of Change*, by William Ayers, Kevin Kumashiro, Erica Meiners, Therese Quinn, and David Stovall, also considers teachers as agents of change on a broader scale. The authors share their ideas about how teachers can better humanize schooling for students, combat some of the current failings of market models of education, and extend their teaching work past the school day and outside the school walls. Their book invites readers into a view of education through the eyes of students, and it provides thoughtful strategies to enact teaching for social justice as not just a popular slogan but an authentic focus on human rights and social equity for all.

And, to close out the series, Book 6, *Making a Difference: Developing Meaningful Careers in Education*, by Karen Hunter Quartz, Brad Olsen, Lauren Anderson, and Kimberly Barraza Lyons, looks at whole careers in education. This book examines the dynamic lives and work of several educators in Los Angeles and investigates why teachers stay in the classroom or shift to other kinds of education roles, such as school administrator, curriculum coordinator, or teacher mentor. The book unpacks the sometimes maddening complexity of the teaching

profession and offers a roadmap for how teachers can, themselves, remain challenged and satisfied as educators without relaxing their commitments to students.

There are different approaches to reading the books in this series.
One way is to consider the whole series as a coherent set of sequenced
conversations about teaching. In this manner, you might read the books
one at a time, all the way through, inserting yourself into the text of the
books: Do the stories and experiences in the books ring true for you?
How will you use these books to improve your practice, broaden your
influence, and deepen your professional satisfaction? You might imagine, as you read the books this way, that you are sitting in a room with
the authors—listening to their ideas, questioning them, actively engaging with their arguments, or talking back to the text when necessary.

Or perhaps you might use these books as textbooks—as thoughtful
primers on selected topics that interest you. In this manner, you might
pick and choose particular chapters to study: Which specific ideas will
you implement in your teaching tomorrow? Are there further readings
or key resources that you will hunt down and look at on your own?
What concrete activities will you try out? Write notes in the margins of
the books and return to the chapters regularly. Photocopy single pages
(not whole chapters, please!) to share with peers. Use the books as you
plan lessons or design curricula. Engage with the reflection questions
at the end of each book's chapters. You will find occasionally in the
margins cross-references on specific topics to other books in the series.
When you read "Cross-Reference, See Book 2 . . ." you can use the
numbered list of titles on p. ii to correlate each reference to the intended book.

Or, you may pick some of the books to read collectively with other
educators—maybe with your teacher education cohort, or as a group of
teachers working with a mentor, or perhaps as part of a teacher inquiry
group that you set up with colleagues. Group discussion of these books
allows their arguments, perspectives, and examples to prompt your own
collective reflection and professional growth: What themes from the
books call out to you? What points might you disagree with? How
might different educators among you interpret parts of these books in
different, perhaps competing, ways? How can these books inspire you
to create specific collaborative projects or teacher networks you can cre-

ate at your school site? You may find the reflection questions at the end
of each chapter particularly useful for group conversation.

This series of books is called the "Teacher's Toolkit," but maybe, for
some, the idea of a *toolkit* for teachers may not, at first glance, be apt.
Picturing a toolkit could conjure images of a steel toolbox or superhero
belt full of hardware for educators—a diagnostic screwdriver, the
clawhammer of homework, a set of precision wrenches for adjusting
student learning on the fly. Such images are, well, just too instrumen-
tal. They risk suggesting that teaching is mechanical or automatic, or
that what good educators do is select utensils from their box to apply
when needed. That doesn't describe the kind of teaching I know and
love. It erroneously suggests that students are to be fastened with bolts
or hammered into obedience, or that learning is gut-wrenchingly rigid.
And, to my mind, such a view treats teachers as technicians trained by
rote, using tools given to them by others, following directions written
on the outside of the box.

Instead, the authors of these books conceive of education as less
fixed, more fluid, less finished, more uncertain, and certainly far more
complicated than anything for which traditional tools would work.
These authors—based on their own years of experience as classroom
teachers, educational researchers, school administrators, and university
professors—view education similarly to how educational philosopher
John Dewey did when, in 1934, he wrote:

> About 40 years ago, a new idea dawned in education. Educators began
> to see that education should parallel life, that the school should repro-
> duce the child's world. In this new type of education the child, instead
> of the curriculum, became the centre of interest, and since the child is
> active, changing, creative—education ceased to be static, [and] became
> dynamic and creative in response to the needs of the child.[1]

Like Dewey, I understand teaching and learning to be context-specific,
highly creative, dynamically student-centered activities that are as
complicated and multifaceted as life itself. And just as important.

So let's reimagine the analogy of a teacher's toolkit. A *toolkit* for teachers could instead be a metaphor for a thoughtful, useful, provocative

bundle of perspectives, theories, and approaches for teachers—a set of lively teaching discussions written by different authors who share some common ground. This bundle would empathize with teachers since its authors are all teachers, as well as education researchers and writers: they know both how difficult and how rewarding teaching can be. But it would also exhort teachers not to fall down on the job—not to shirk their work, make excuses, or lessen their resolve to support students.

The bundle of teaching conversations could share stories from the classroom that reveal teaching to be kaleidoscopic: made up of thousands of shifting views, hundreds of competing relations, and dozens of different ways to succeed with children. The stories would reveal how to be a great teacher and why doing so is so damned important. The bundle of ideas and perspectives would include actual examples of good teaching, lesson ideas, and lots of research tidbits useful for prospective and practicing educators. Yes, that could be a toolkit I would want to own. It would be a kit full of thoughtful perspectives, research summaries, wisdom of practice, and impassioned words of advice from handpicked educationalists. An "idea-kit," really. A boxed set of thoughtful primers on how to teach well for social change in the current global climate.

John Dewey famously built binaries in his writing—teaching is either this or that; students learn in this way but not in that way—only to collapse the binary in the end and suggest that education is too complicated for easy contradictions. So I'll take a page from Dewey's playbook and attempt the same. Maybe we can consider this book series as not an either/or. Not as *either* a box of teaching instruments *or* a collection of thoughtful conversations about education, but as both: a set of tangible strategies for teachers to make their own and a loosely bundled collection of professional arguments for use by educators in order to think for themselves, but in deeper and newer ways than before. That's the way that I prefer to envision this teacher's toolkit.

No matter how you choose to make use of the books in the Teacher's Toolkit, it is our sincere hope that you will find value in them. We have tried to make them accessible, conversational, substantive, and succinct. We all believe that teaching is a fundamentally important profession, and, if this world is to improve and grow, it will be because our teachers can help future generations to become wise, creative, and critical thinkers who put their ideas into action toward improving the societies they will inherit. You are an essential part of that human process.

—Brad Olsen
University of California, Santa Cruz

NOTE

1. Dewey, J. 1934. "Tomorrow May Be too Late: Save the Schools Now." Reprinted in J. Boydston (ed.) 1986 *John Dewey: The Later Works, 1925–1953: 1933–1934, Vol. 9.* Carbondale, I: Southern Illinois University Press. 386.

ACKNOWLEDGMENTS

I AM PARTICULARLY indebted to the teachers who agreed to be interviewed for this book. Their generosity and patience helped me to understand more deeply something I thought I already knew. Countless thanks to Brad Olsen and Paradigm Publishers for their guidance and support throughout this process and to Lauren Anderson for being a critical friend. I am deeply thankful for Nikole's constant support of and insight into this book's content as well as its author, for the rest of my family's consistent encouragement, and finally for Olivia, who personifies the powerful potential of smallness.

INTRODUCTION

MOST HIGH SCHOOLS—large and small—
seek to provide challenging academics, strong
teaching, and a healthy school climate so that
their students can successfully graduate. Their teachers
work countless hours, inside and outside the classroom,
to do the best job they can. And while all teachers have
the same goal (to help their students succeed), each
teacher works in a different school context—within a
unique physical space and political environment, and
among unique administrators, students, and colleagues.
Each teacher decides how she will negotiate the harmony
or discord between that context and her own vision of
how children best learn and how teachers best teach. For
example, teachers make adjustments to accommodate the
layout and architectural idiosyncrasies of their classrooms. They ignore or acquiesce to the mercurial demands of a poor administrator and capitalize on the
support of an effective one. They connect with or separate themselves from their colleagues based on professional and personal similarities. They approach certain
aspects of their curriculum gingerly or with zest depending on the political views and beliefs of their school's
families. The savvy and resourceful teacher may be able

**Cross-Reference
For more on
preparing an
ideal learning
environment,
see Book 5,
Chapter 1.**

to manage and mitigate the effects of these characteristics on her day-to-day practice. After all, she can simply shut her classroom door.

But the size of the school is different. It matters.

Some effects of a large student body seem obvious: the larger size of the cafeteria and parking lot, the more band marchers during halftime, the greater fundraising capacity of the PTA. And it may seem that more students in a school would not really have an impact on a teacher's experience—especially if her class size is unchanged—except to make pep rallies and fire drills more challenging to supervise and to increase the number of teachers in a faculty meeting (hopefully not increasing its length!). While every teacher is somewhat affected by her school and classroom context, some might assume that school size, like the length of the lunch period or the number of windows in the room, is simply part of the occupational terrain each teacher negotiates but does not fundamentally affect a teacher's approach to her work.

In fact, depending on the number of students enrolled, a school can facilitate, promote, impede, and prohibit specific types of teacher practices and educational experiences. In other words, the size of the school powerfully influences how educators work and the decisions they make. It has prevailing effects on, and is a reflection of, how the school's surrounding community approaches its educative function.

One of my first experiences in a small high school was in the mid-1990s, when I visited the Julia Richman Education Complex on East Sixty-Eighth Street in New York City. Julia Richman High School had been a large comprehensive school, but now JREC was a facility that housed six small schools, each occupying one floor of a building and serving no more than 400 students. On entering the building, one of the first things I noticed was not the physical space, the number of students, or the teachers. It was the bells, or rather, I noticed that there were no bells. In each small school within JREC, the students seemed to intuitively, as if of one mind, leave class-rooms at around the same time for passing period and ar-rive at their next class at generally the same time a few minutes later, when the hallways would be empty. The lack of interruptions by the bells also seemed more like the real world. What kinds of schools were these?

Before that visit, I hadn't known that public high schools could be small. As a teenager in Omaha, Ne-braska, my high school had 1,500 students in grades 10–12. It was, as I learned much later, a fairly traditional model of high schools in the United States, with eight fifty-minute periods and four minutes between each class. With 1,500 students, I knew many by name and more by face, and knew best the students in my classes; because I was in the honors track, we thirty students es-sentially moved together from class to class throughout the day. By senior year I knew most of the students in my grade and a handful of students in other grades, usually if they were in one of my elective classes, like jazz band, or in an extracurricular sport or club. I knew some of my teachers better than others, knew my counselor fairly well, and didn't know the principal or assistant principal at all. I didn't really think much about whether my expe-riences were any different from my peers' in the school, but I like to think that's typical for a teenager.

Several years after my experience as a high school stu-dent, I taught in a comprehensive high school in Georgia. I was one teacher among a staff of seventy-five or so, and taught five classes of about thirty students each day—some remedial classes, some "regular" classes, and some honors classes, primarily composed of students in the school's magnet program. My first year, I assigned compli-cated assignments that I (and I hoped the students) found to be valuable and authentic learning experiences—a rookie mistake, for the assignments took so much time to grade that I was lucky if I returned students' corrected as-signments before the end of the semester. I quickly learned that a large part of being a teacher was managing my workload—if I was going to give an assignment to 150 students, the assignment needed to be easy for me to correct, which also generally made it easier for the students to complete.

Also that first year, I naively thought I could get to know all of my students well—I attempted to visit each of their homes and meet their families, an ambitious practice that lasted until the end of October, when I ran out of both time and psychological energy. I eventually resigned myself to the idea that I couldn't get to know all of my students. A handful of students I got to know fairly well; I learned their academic strengths and weaknesses and could make adjustments and provide supports and challenges, usually outside of class (for example, by tutoring or offering a book that they would like). Through that relationship I sometimes learned about their struggles with peers, parents, and their futures, and was able to give my two cents or cut them a break when I could tell they were having a bad day. Sometimes I was even able to meet their families and see their neighborhoods. But these opportunities were few. Out of a daily student load of 150, I knew maybe a few dozen well. For those, perhaps I was able to be the kind of teacher I had always wanted to be. For the rest, I was the adult authority who gave assignments, and they were the ones who were expected to complete those assignments. My students seemed to respect me and the work we did, and most passed my class. I was a popular teacher—I won the school's "Most Creative Teacher" award and the dubious accolade of "Most Likely to Give Homework on the Weekend"—and was honored at the state level.

Nevertheless, two aspects of my work troubled me. First, some students didn't pass my class or do well in school, and I didn't have the time to understand their needs. It may have been learning styles that I couldn't identify, distractions they had outside my class or outside the school, or skill gaps, but I wasn't able to figure out what the problem was. Maybe they weren't successful because I simply hadn't made the class interesting enough, I hypothesized. I consoled myself with the belief that I had done everything I could—I could only lead the horses to water—and that I was only a single teacher within a whole school. Maybe just as I had connected with and knew a handful of students, every teacher knew a different handful. I had to trust that another teacher was establishing relationships and understanding those students I hadn't connected with, although there wasn't any way I could confirm this assumption.

Second, I was concerned that my interaction with my colleagues mirrored my work with students. I knew only a few of the other teachers well, primarily because I really didn't have a chance to interact with them. Department and faculty meetings were generally packed with administrative tasks; we were asked to implement new policies or procedures, hear announcements, or sing "Happy Birthday" for that month. The discussions I had with other teachers about teaching and learning occurred informally, squeezed into a passing period or during lunch; sometimes I walked next door to a social studies teacher's or chemistry teacher's classroom to share a frustrating experience or to brainstorm an idea. There were few times when the school carved out time expecting and guiding us to learn from each other. These two concerns overlapped when I struggled with a student. Did other teachers have information about that student—who she was or how she learned—that I could use? Similarly, when I was succeeding with a student who was failing in other teachers' classes, I had information about the student and had implemented successful strategies that would benefit the student if other teachers knew what I did. Yet there was no system or culture in the school in which teachers could share individual knowledge to strengthen our collective efforts. I sometimes wondered what it meant that although we were all supposed to teach, we weren't given many ways to listen to or learn from each other.

In the school's magnet program, however, things were different. There students seemed connected to each other and to their teachers, and teachers worked with each other to co-plan program-wide themes, solve problems related to the students they worked with, or develop cross-disciplinary instructional activities. By contrast, we teachers outside the magnet program essentially were on our own. For some reason, though, when the teachers within the magnet tried to include the school's entire student body in their activities, it just didn't seem to work for either the teachers or the students.

Looking back, I believe our entire staff knew that significant groups of students weren't being served in our school, but it was as if we were working with unknown and unspoken constraints on us and our students, and there wasn't anything we could do about it. It didn't seem that the administration was deliberately creating this environment; it just seemed to be the way it had always been and the only way it could be. Our school was a collection of teachers with no agreed-on vision, pedagogy, or beliefs, who worked in their individual classrooms and closed their doors. We all did the best we could, each in our own unique way.

These two frustrations—students' disconnection from teachers and teachers' isolation from each other—led me to a temporary stopover in law school (which seemed like a good idea at the time). But I immediately missed high school students and the dynamics of a high school classroom, as well as my intermittent conversations with fellow teachers about teaching and learning, so while in law school I enrolled concurrently in an administration certification program. It was within this program that I visited three schools in the Julia Richman complex—Vanguard High School, Urban Academy, and Manhattan International High School, schools that had a reputation for succeeding with students in ways that other high schools weren't. Visiting different kinds of high schools, I thought, would help me understand different job options as well as inform my thinking of how high schools can succeed. At each school, I sat in classes and spoke with the schools' leaders, teachers, and students. The more I saw and listened, the more I realized that it wasn't just the lack of bells that defined these schools.

The teachers in these small high schools weren't much different from my colleagues in Georgia; they were passionate, loved working with teenagers, and were constantly trying to better their craft. But here interactions among teachers and students were structured in ways that were unfamiliar to me but that made all the sense in the world. Teachers were organized into teams responsible for a small number of students, similar to a middle school model. Each team knew their collective students very well; they shared information they learned about students and strategies they found successful so they could help each other be more effective. With this common insight, they could anticipate aspects of assignments that would give certain students difficulty, and therefore tailor assignments to meet students' needs or capitalize on their strengths; they could advise students to approach tasks with a particular strategy or group struggling students with others for assistance. Teachers also seemed to know their colleagues well enough to trust and depend on each other. Nearly every discussion was intended to be or quickly evolved into sharing information about students, seeking advice on a dilemma, reviewing student work, or undertaking a new curricular initiative across classes or schoolwide.

Students seemed to be having different experiences as well. In classrooms, they worked collaboratively on assignments, seemed more invested in the work they were doing, and wanted not only to succeed for themselves but to make their teachers and even their peers proud of them. The teenagers also seemed less cliquish and less segregated, interacting with students with whom they had nothing in common—some of which may have been due to the polyglot nature of New York City, but it was still something that rarely happened in the high schools I was in as a student or teacher. Just as the teachers knew students well, so the students seemed to know each other.

And while each of the schools within the building had those similarities, each school also had a unique culture that was immediate and obvious. At one school, a student walked through the hall ringing a loud bell to signify that she had completed a benchmark requirement: the humanities element of her academic portfolio. Another school had student artwork covering nearly every inch of wall space. At another, they considered themselves a global community of non-English-speaking students learning English together. The schools weren't identifiable by a mascot (in fact, I don't even remember them having sports teams, much less mascots) but forged an identity through an academic theme or approach to learning.

In each of these schools, the small number of students and teachers seemed to make a difference. There was a familiarity, almost an intimacy, among the adults and students that changed how they approached teaching and learning. Teachers used what they knew about students to help them learn, and students worked closely with teachers to produce work that required deeper thinking and allowed for greater investment and creativity. Students and teachers seemed guided and driven by a purposefulness and meaning to their work. At the time, I didn't fully understand how or why the size of the school mattered, but I was certain that these schools had been able to do something that the large schools I had been in had been unable to do. My colleagues in Georgia hadn't seemed any less committed or less visionary, just less connected to students and to each other.

Since those visits ten years ago, I have worked almost entirely with or in small high schools at the site and district levels. I have been the founding principal of a small high school, the principal of a turnaround small school, a director in New York City's Office of Small Schools, and a consultant for groups seeking to create small schools. What I have learned boils down to the following:

1. Certain powerful teaching and learning opportunities that are possible in small high schools are generally unlikely to occur in large high schools.

2. Conversely, large schools are able to offer certain experiences that are simply not possible in small schools.

3. Small schools do not guarantee more effective teaching and learning opportunities simply because of their size but require deliberate structures and intentional practices.

In other words, large and small schools offer opportunities for fundamentally different experiences, for teachers as well as their students. The size of the school isn't something that teachers simply manage and adjust to; the school size can define their work conditions, possibilities for instruction, and what it means to be a teacher.

WHAT WE TALK ABOUT WHEN WE TALK ABOUT A SMALL HIGH SCHOOL

Research in the last decade has generally agreed that a school is small—able to create certain conditions not found in large schools—when the student body is between 400 and 800 students (Raywid 1999). This book will focus on the experiences of teachers in small *public* high schools, but the impact of school size is true regardless of whether the school is privately or publicly funded. It is certainly not a coincidence that most private high schools, including those most selective and prestigious, are small: the average private high school enrolls 360 students. By contrast, the average public high school enrolls

811 students (NCES 2007), and it is not unusual for high school students to attend schools with upwards of 2,000 to 4,000 students, which raises the following question: what is it about small high schools that the most privileged in our society are willing to pay for, but that the public sphere seems resistant to provide?

Why limit this book to the high school? First, there are relatively few large elementary or middle schools that fit the definition of "large" when compared with high school populations. In most districts, many elementary schools feed into several larger middle schools that feed into a handful of even larger high schools. While most of the dynamics of small high schools would be found in small middle schools or elementary schools, it is high schools for which being small is the most unusual. Small high schools are therefore worth specific exploration.

Second, states' compulsory education laws usually end for children when they are between sixteen and eighteen years old, making high schools the final opportunity for our government to provide young citizens with the preparation they need to pursue postsecondary opportunities or household-supporting jobs. It is also in high school that enrollment essentially becomes optional, when students "age out" of school, so it is particularly important that we create high schools in which students find meaning and value in their learning experiences.

Most importantly, our collective failure to serve all adolescents through high school graduation is a national concern. According to a report by Editorial Projects in Education, only 71 percent of our public school students graduate from high school (Editorial Projects in Education 2008). In raw numbers, approximately 1.2 million high school students in the United States drop out each year, averaging a stunning 7,000 per day, who immediately seek to enter a workforce to which they generally can offer only a limited contribution (Editorial Projects in Education 2007). High school dropouts in the United States account for 13 percent of the adult population, but less than 6 percent of the dollars earned (Swanson 2009, 13). Each dropout, over her lifetime, costs our nation approximately $260,000 in unearned income (Rouse 2005). The Alliance for Excellent Education calculated that, based on state-by-state dropout statistics, almost 13 million students will drop out over the next decade, resulting in a loss to our national economy of over $3 trillion (2009). The problem is of such magnitude that, for what was surely the first time in history, our president chose to address those who would consider dropping out of high school in a speech to a joint session of Congress, imploring them: "Dropping out of high school is no longer an option. It's not just quitting on yourself; it's quitting on your country" (Obama 2009). President Obama was addressing us educators as well: we must find ways to make our high schools places where students don't want to drop out—where young people are cared for, believed in, and equipped to be productive members of our society.

WHAT WE'VE LEARNED ABOUT SMALL VERSUS LARGE SCHOOLS

Small schools have been a part of the American educational landscape since our country's inception, but the modern small high school movement has gained momentum in the last two decades, contributing to and drawing upon a growing body of evidence that small schools offer significant benefits. As Kathleen Cotton, reviewing years of research, studies, reviews, and reports, found, "Research over the past 15 years has convincingly demonstrated that small schools are superior to large ones on many measures and equal to them on the rest" (2001, 1).

The research that Cotton refers to and the meta-analyses of that research have consistently found that small schools engender among students a greater sense of belonging and attachment, are safer, and have lower dropout rates, higher attendance rates, and lower suspension rates (Cotton 1996; Ayers, Bracey, and Smith 2000; Wasley et al. 2000). There is significant, although not yet conclusive, evidence of a correlation between small schools and higher student achievement. Most research has found that students in small schools have improved student test scores, increased learning, and higher graduation rates compared with students in large schools (e.g., Fowler and Walberg 1991; Lee and Smith 1997; Wasley et al. 2000; Howley and Howley 2004), while some studies have indicated that a direct relationship between school size and student achievement is less secure (e.g., Lee 2004; Kahne et al. 2008). What the research does seem to agree on is that a school's "size acts as a facilitating or debilitating factor for other organizational forms or practices that, in turn, promote student learning" (Lee and Smith 1997, 218).

As a result of this research, the small school model has been endorsed by the National Education Association, the United Federation of Teachers, and the National Association of Secondary School Principals, which has made "smallness" an essential element of effective schools, stating that high schools "must break into units of no more than 600 students." In 2002, the National Conference of State Legislatures published a statement endorsing small schools, stating the following benefits borne out by research:

- Smaller schools support academic achievement.
- Smaller schools promote academic equity.
- Student attitudes and behavior are more positive in smaller schools.
- Extracurricular participation rates are higher in smaller schools.
- Attendance is higher and dropout rates lower in smaller schools.
- Students feel better about themselves and others in smaller schools.

- Smaller schools prepare students for college as well as or better than larger schools.
- Larger schools reach a point of diminishing returns on cost-effectiveness.

Chicago, Boston, and New York City have become well-known for their small-school initiatives and have made significant contributions to our understanding of the benefits and challenges of teaching in small high schools. Chicago implemented its High School Redesign Initiative in 2001, redesigning three large underperforming high schools into twelve small schools and developing another twelve entirely new small schools. Boston created a set of "pilot schools" in 1994 out of a partnership between the Boston School District and its teachers' union. Under a separate union contract, pilot-school staff are granted increased autonomy over budget, staffing, governance, curriculum and assessment, and the school calendar. In New York City, the small schools movement began in the mid-1980s with the establishment of Central Park East Secondary School, then grew during the 1990s through a public-private partnership between the New York City Board of Education, the Center for Collaborative Education, and the nonprofit Fund for New York City Public Education that established thirty-two small high schools. This movement has evolved into the City's Empowerment Schools initiative, which now includes over three hundred small high schools. Though these initiatives have been heavily scrutinized, and have not been unequivocal successes on all measures, in all three cities the small high schools, as compared with the larger preexisting high schools, have shown better attendance, lower dropout rates, greater student and parent satisfaction, and in many cases stronger student achievement (Wasley et al. 2000; Center for Collaborative Education 2006). Size matters: as we will explore throughout this book, though a school being small does not in itself guarantee academic success, it is in a small school that conditions for that success are most possible.

THE PURPOSE OF THIS BOOK

Most of the books about small high schools are school profiles—for example, Eliot Levine's *One Kid at a Time: Big Lessons from a Small School* (2002), describing the Met School in Providence, Rhode Island, and *The Power of Their Ideas: Lessons for America from a Small School in Harlem* by Deborah Meier (1995), about the development of Central Park East Secondary School in Harlem—or how-to books for those who want to create a small school or small learning environment—for example, Alan Blanchard and Brooke Harms's *Transforming the High School Experience: The Practitioner's Guide to Small Learning Communities* (2006). Both of these genres focus primarily on how the small size of schools can affect students' experiences. Less has been written about how smallness affects teachers' professional experiences—their interactions with students, colleagues, administrators, families, and the outside communities.

For LaRavian Battle, an algebra teacher in a small school in Oakland, transitioning from a large school into a small school has changed the nature of her work, even changing her self-conception of what it is to be a teacher:

> In the large school, I was a teacher. I talked to my parents, I talked to my students, occasionally I talked with the counselor, but that's all I had to do. I kept my door closed, and I handled whatever was happening in my classroom. The rest of the school was somebody else's problem and somebody else's job. . . . As my student body got smaller, my job got bigger because I had to do so much more—helping with the master schedule, helping with the student schedule—even when we had to hire a teacher, I was on the interview board. Students

might need after-school tutoring, so we had to make sure that if it's not me [to provide it], then who?

This book will explain the dynamics of being a teacher in a small school: what having fewer students in a school means for your students, fellow teachers, administrators, families, and community; what being part of a small school enables you and your fellow educators to potentially, but by no means necessarily, provide for students and yourselves; and what aspects of smallness teachers can advocate for in their school regardless of its size. We will see that while the large high school uses bells and other depersonalized systems to manage experiences and behaviors of students and teachers, the small high school generally doesn't need or want bells, and not just because there are fewer students. Small schools are organized so that people know each other as individuals; this means that teaching and learning are not driven by the need to maximize efficiencies but motivated by the powerful educational potential inherent in personalized learning experiences.

Throughout this book, I will draw upon research, professional experiences, and the words of teachers to describe structures, priorities, and dynamics in large and small schools that either impede or facilitate greater student success and higher satisfaction of the teachers who intend that success. We will also see how large schools, because of their organizational structures and institutional dynamics, are less likely to offer the conditions for effective teacher practice.

Though not yet ubiquitous throughout the country, small high schools are becoming a real employment option for teachers. If you are about to enter the teaching job market or are an experienced teacher considering a change in school, the information in this book will equip you to make a more educated decision about whether and why you might want (or not want) to teach in a small school. Most of us who attended public high schools as students did so in large schools—by which I mean over 1,000 students—so small schools are unfamiliar and easy to dismiss for not being "real" high schools. When a community offers different high school options, just as families and students must find the school that best fits them, it is not only important but critical that you as a teaching professional affirmatively choose to work in a school where you believe you can do your most effective work and where you will be most fulfilled. It is crucial that a teacher seeking a job recognizes attributes of large and small high schools and aligns her beliefs with the appropriate school size.

But this book is not just for the new teacher or one exploring new teaching opportunities in communities that offer both small and large high schools. Teachers at any point in their careers can reexamine the structural conditions of their work and become informed reformers of their own schools. This book will help you separate small schools' rhetoric from small schools' realities so you can deepen your understanding about what small schools potentially offer teachers who work in them. And this book is not only for teachers. Every reader—from researcher to policymaker to parent—who understands the promising practices and professional norms that have been nurtured under conditions of smallness can become an agent of change in public education.

This book will take you into small schools and their teaching and learning spaces—classrooms as well as hallways. You will learn about what it means to be a small-school teacher and do "small-school teaching," which requires a critical, collaborative, progressive professionalism. You will learn about small schools from research as well as through the voices of educators like LaRavian who have chosen to teach there; they share what teaching in a small school has meant for their relationships, practices, and professional lives.

LaRavian is one of seven practitioners in small high schools whom I interviewed to inform my writing and whose stories I share. These teachers in small schools, all highly regarded by their colleagues, will help us learn how the conditions of small schools make powerful teaching practices more possible. Because this is not a systematic research project, it seems unnecessary to give complete introductions for each of them, but a description of the group is appropriate:

- All currently or previously worked in small high schools. Of those, five had formerly taught in large comprehensive schools.
- They represent California; Washington, DC; Colorado; Texas; or New York.
- Their teaching experience ranges from seven to fifteen years.
- They currently are or have been teachers or teacher-leaders.

For a list of interview participants see References.

But I also wanted to understand how successful teachers in large schools negotiate their schools' size and provide effective instruction. To do so I interviewed several teachers in large comprehensive high schools who have been identified as Teacher of the Year by their state or, in one case, the nation. All currently work in high schools with at least 1,800 students, and they represent California, Kansas, Montana, or Minnesota. You will hear how these teachers exhibit small-school behaviors, often on their own and despite the large school not being oriented to support those strategies. Although small schools are uniquely able to facilitate certain teaching and learning experiences for students and teachers, this book will draw on the stories of those teachers to provide specific small-school practices and strategies that teachers in large schools can implement.

I am indebted to all those I interviewed; their experiences and insight deepened my understanding of smallness in unanticipated and challenging ways. I am awed and humbled by their work.

Chapter 1 will describe how the majority of our nation's public high schools are cast in an image created in the nineteenth century, with a design and structure that reflect priorities, interests, and philosophies of a different country from the one we live in today. With its emphasis on efficiency and specialization, the large high school creates environments that are depersonalized and orderly, and encourages teachers to focus only on their own classrooms. Students are given many choices (some of which are forced choices) that result in different learning experiences and that ultimately yield varying qualities of preparation for post–high school opportunities. Both teachers and students, in the midst of large numbers of people, essentially work and learn alone.

Subsequent chapters focus on teachers' experiences in small high schools. As opposed to large schools' emphasis on impersonal efficiencies, small schools are organized around relationships and personalization. Chapter 2 explains how the small-high-school teacher is able to build relationships with her students and how these relationships change the teaching and learning experiences both inside and outside her classroom. Chapter 3 explores how teachers in small schools build relationships with each other that foster what Judith Warren Little calls "joint work" (1990, 519)—authentic and constructive collaboration—across subjects and grades. We will see that because small schools facilitate collaboration among teachers, students' learning experiences can become more meaningful and coherent within and across different subjects. Chapter 4 discusses the expanded and empowering roles that teachers in small schools often play beyond their classrooms, which puts them in a very different relationship with each other and the school's administration from what they might experience within the large school's traditional organizational hierarchy. Finally, Chapter 5 examines additional challenges for teachers in small schools and how large schools, amid their own challenges, attempt to become small.

Because one targeted group of readers for this book is new teachers, I thought it would be helpful to open each chapter with an excerpt of the journal I kept during my first year of teaching in the Georgia comprehensive high school where I taught English and U.S. history. I use these journal entries to frame the chapter and to highlight how I, as a new teacher, experienced and reflected on my work in a comprehensive school.

One additional point to keep in mind while you read this book: even though our predominant and century-old model for public high schools clearly fails to meet the needs of unacceptable numbers of young people, and the most prestigious and expensive high school education is provided by small private schools, too many of us have willfully ignored, or worse dismissed, the possibilities of small-school design for children in public schools as well as for ourselves as public school teachers. We stick our heads in the sand even though research has found that the larger the school, the lower the students' achievement levels, particularly for historically underserved groups. As Craig Howley found in his survey of decades of research on the relationship of school size to student achievement: "Nothing in the empirically based research literature on school size and achievement suggests that academic benefits of any sort accrue in schools larger than this [1,000 students], even schools serving a very affluent clientele" (Howley 2002, 65). When the superiority of small schools has been proven "with a clarity and at a level of confidence rare in the annals of education research" (Raywid 1999), how can we justify a comprehensive high school model that clearly limits students' opportunities to succeed?

Being more informed about what is possible and often facilitated in small schools will enable us as educators to

better reflect on our own practices, consider certain pedagogical strategies against the organizational characteristics
of schools, and make educated career choices. Educators
and researchers can develop more focused advocacy efforts, become more discerning consumers of press coverage and policy rhetoric, and be more empowered to
improve our public high schools—whether by redesigning them into small schools or by transplanting and trans-
lating small-school practices and strategies. In other
words, perhaps learning about small schools, if not
changing where teachers choose to work, will change how
they work wherever they are. Teachers in large schools,
having learned about the experiences of teachers in small
schools, could find ways to adapt and transfer those practices to their own setting, aiming to reduce the *experienced*
size of the school. That alone may be enough to make a
course correction in our nation's approach to secondary
education. We can no longer be forgiven for ignoring the
opportunities in small schools, for our students' sake as
well as our own.

In other words, let's reconsider whether we need to
continue teaching with bells.

CHAPTER ONE

LARGE AND SMALL HIGH SCHOOLS

Some Key Comparisons

FROM MY JOURNAL during my first year of teaching:

I know I should keep my emotions and opinions in check in front of the students, especially when it comes to the school's policies, but I couldn't help it today.

It was toward the end of the period, and the students and I were having a great discussion about whether Black History Month is important in order to celebrate African American history and culture, or whether having that celebration be assigned to a single month gives people an excuse to not value or discuss African American history and culture the rest of the year. I was keeping an eye on the time, wanting to make sure that as I facilitated the discussion, certain topics were addressed and that all students had a chance to speak, when the PA system came on. The secretary made an announcement that the soccer team's practice was cancelled, but that there would be a brief meeting in the coach's classroom. Then she repeated the announcement. And then the bell rang ending the period. I felt so defeated. I had been holding the chalkboard eraser and threw it at the speakerbox on the wall in frustration.

As students got up to leave, some students laughed at my frustration, others seemed shocked by my reaction, and a few stopped to console me, suggesting that we could continue the discussion tomorrow. Of course, I had already planned out my lesson for tomorrow, and we had to move on. I felt defeated—what was the point of carefully planning a lesson if it could be interrupted, and by an announcement that affected only about two dozen students? What message did that send to the students about what was important? What message did it send to us teachers?

A SHORT HISTORY OF THE COMPREHENSIVE HIGH SCHOOL

Future chapters will dive deeply into small-school structures and experiences of teachers there, but a preliminary discussion of large schools is important. The comprehensive high school seems familiar to most of us, either because we attended them as students or worked there as adults or because they are part of Americans' collective nostalgia, a setting for nearly every novel, television show, and film that involves teenagers. Yet few are aware of how the twenty-first century's comprehensive high school has nearly the same design as it did in the early twentieth century, when it was created to prepare students for an entirely different world and, many believe, it had priorities and purposes that have become obsolete, inappropriate, and—to some—unacceptable.

We begin with a brief history of the comprehensive high school in the United States, borrowed from David Tyack's *The One Best System*. Schools in America's first century had been almost uniformly small, especially by contemporary standards. With the nation's population scattered throughout rural areas, one-room schoolhouses served multiple grades and shifting subsets of students depending on the season, family obligations, and perceived value of an "academic" education. Few experienced high schools as a separate unit of education; in 1890 just over 220,000 students attended 2,526 high schools, and only for an average of eighty-six days a year. Half of the high schools enrolled fewer than 100 students, and the curriculum was entirely college preparatory (Tyack 1974, 32–33).

In the mid- to late 1800s, with the growth in America's industrialization, an influx of immigrants, and the migration of American citizens from rural settlements, the number of people living in urban areas increased 800 percent. As city populations grew, the government had two overlapping needs: to provide a coherent and efficient administration of city services—transportation, safety, health, commerce, and education—and to prepare the emerging adults of each city to successfully enter the workplace. These needs and concerns intersected in public school systems.

Up until the first half of the nineteenth century, schools had been run essentially as distinct units, each with its own governance committee. Because the nation's population had been living in primarily rural areas, it had not been a priority, or even a possibility, to organize and govern schools within a single education system. As cities grew and industrialization fueled the nation's economic, social, and political engines, policymakers applied the economic principles of efficiency and specialization to other aspects of society. In education, the intent seemed a blend of democracy and economics: all schools within a city should provide a uniform educational experience to their students. No longer would there be a disjointed school system with disparate opportunities, but instead an educational bureaucracy, managed by a superintendent, would consolidate all schools under a single set of policies, curriculum, and school design.

By the 1920s, as social progressives succeeded in creating common educational opportunities for broader segments of the population (although often excluding African Americans), as compulsory attendance laws were taken more seriously, and as cities and their factories grew, the number of middle and secondary schools increased. While the nation's total population increased only 68 percent between 1890 and 1918, enrollment in high schools increased so rapidly—by 711 percent—that an average of one new high school was built each day (Tyack 1974, 183). Suddenly, high schools were enrolling nearly 80 percent of the fourteen- to seventeen-year-old population.

But what was the common education that students experienced in high schools? Tyack writes that in the late nineteenth century, schools in cities were intended to "inculcate obedience to bureaucratic norms overtly and with zest" (1974, 49). The curriculum's emphases were punctuality, obedience, precision, and silence. During this time, few employers needed employees to be high school graduates, so except for bright children whose families could survive financially without their labor, the teenage years needed to be a smooth transition from the classroom to the factory. The school therefore needed to incorporate elements of the factory floor so that students could be prepared for that work.

In addition, just as all specialized jobs in the factory, working together, made for maximum efficiency in production, schools sorted students according to perceived ability and provided them with what educators believed was most appropriate for their lot in life. High schools often grouped their courses into different tracks, commonly called "college," "commercial," "vocational," and "general" (Tyack and Cuban 1995, 48). In 1917, the Federal Commission on the Reorganization of Secondary Education, in its widely read publication "Cardinal Principles," wrote that the high school should offer different educational opportunities for students of "widely varying capacities, aptitudes, social heredity, and destinies in life" (Tyack and Cuban 1995, 51). In other words, the high school should be "comprehensive" in its offerings. (A **comprehensive high school** intends to provide a vast array of different courses, programs, and resources to accommodate the diversity of student interests and the perceived variances in students' academic capacities.) It was in this context that such comprehensive large schools became widespread, each intending to serve all students by providing multiple and differentiated academic tracks.

Key concept
comprehensive high school

A large high school, therefore, was clearly superior to a small one for implementing the philosophical priorities of the twentieth-century school: Americanization, social Darwinism, and efficiencies. *Large schools could mirror the strengths of efficient factories, effectively acculturating and assimilating varied groups of students within the same building, sorting them, and providing differentiated curricula based on perceived ability and need.* And with fewer schools, each serving larger populations, the centralized city bureaucracy could more easily manage the site administrators and the curriculum.

Focus point

This movement explains how the size of high schools grew so dramatically. From 1929 to 1980, the number of students attending public secondary schools increased from 4.4 million to 13.2 million, an astonishing 200 percent increase (NCES 2008, Table 3). Over the same period, the number of public schools serving secondary grades (7–12) increased from 23,930 to only 24,362, a meager 1.8 percent increase (NCES 2008, Table 87), and the number of one-room schools plummeted from 130,000 in 1930 to fewer than 1,000 by 1980 (Tyack and Cuban 1995, 19). These statistics indicate that the number of students in each middle and/or high school rose significantly. Since that time, the size of most high schools has continued to remain large; from 1980 to

2007, the number of public secondary schools in the United States and the number of students served each grew by about 18 percent (29,400 serving 15 million students) (NCES 2008, Tables 3 and 87).

As the size of public secondary schools, particularly high schools, continued to increase through the mid- and late twentieth century, they not only prepared workers for the factory by sorting the students but also replicated many of the values and behaviors promoted by the Industrial Revolution's factory. Throughout the first half of the twentieth century, the interest in teaching students to follow "bureaucratic norms overtly and with zest" remained a priority. Tyack quotes William T. Harris, the superintendent of schools in St. Louis and the future U.S. commissioner of education and "outstanding intellectual leader in American education" in the 1960s, who stated, "The first requisite of the school is Order: each pupil must be taught first and foremost to conform his behavior to a general standard . . . conformity to the time of the train, to the starting of work in the manufactory" (Tyack 1974, 43). As the majority of cities' public school students were being prepared not for postsecondary education but for work in factories, there was a societal interest in teaching them behaviors in which they could flourish in factory culture. A policy paper cosigned by seventy-seven college presidents and city and state superintendents of schools stated that "military precision is required in the maneuvering of classes." The authors continued: "Great stress is laid upon (1) punctuality, (2) regularity, (3) attention, and (4) silence, as habits necessary through life for successful combination with one's fellow-men in an industrial and commercial civilization" (Tyack 1974, 50).

Harris also stated: "The pupil must have his lessons ready at the appointed time, must rise at the tap of the bell, move to the line, return; in short, go through all of the evolutions with equal precision" (Tyack 1974, 43). These were the same bells I heard throughout my time in high schools as a student and teacher, and these schools had been so successful inculcating me that I hadn't even imagined high schools without bells until I walked into my first small school. Tyack describes how the comprehensive school's acculturation of young people to factory life included not only bells but competition for extrinsic rewards (such as grades), adaptation to bureaucratic definitions (being part of a grade level), and conformity to authority with bureaucratic procedures (requiring a hall pass to leave the classroom and use the restroom) (1974, 49).

Just as raw material in a factory underwent a series of specific, specialized manipulations by a series of workers in order to be refined into a finished product, so students progressed through a series of classes, each taught by a teacher specializing in a subject area, intending to produce a finished student. Andy Hargreaves, in his book *Changing Teachers, Changing Times* (1994), states that modern school systems "emerged as factory-like systems of mass education designed to meet the needs of manufacturing and heavy industry. They processed pupils in batches, segregated them into age-graded cohorts called classes or standards, taught them a standardized course or curriculum, and did this through teacher-centered methods of lecturing, recitation, question-and-answer and seatwork" (27). These century-old structures are part of the comprehensive high school's "hidden curriculum" and have persisted and become so ubiquitous that they are accepted without question as the bread and butter of high school environments. The **hidden curriculum** is a school's rules and expectations for students and adults that are never made explicit in course catalogues or in curriculum guides but are systematically enforced.

Key concept
hidden curriculum

In the rest of this chapter, we will learn more about how the design and organizational structure of the early twentieth-century high school and the Industrial Revolution's values—order, efficiency, and specialization— remain in the DNA of the twenty-first-century high

The Industrial Revolution's values—order, efficiency, and specialization—remain in the DNA of the twenty-first-century high school.

school and circumscribe decisions, behaviors, and opportunities for teachers and students in large high schools today.

IMPORTANT CHARACTERISTICS OF LARGE HIGH SCHOOLS

All high schools express priorities of order, efficiency, and specialization in four ways:

1. Communication methods
2. Student groupings
3. Student choices and opportunities
4. Teachers' work contexts

Below I discuss these ways first in the context of large high schools and then in the context of small high schools.

Communication Methods

Focus point

Schools with large student populations require large facilities covering many acres, many floors, or both. *Messages that need to be communicated are sent in broad and impersonal ways that are disturbingly reminiscent of the nineteenth-century factory.* In the Industrial Revolution's factory, bells identified starting and stopping times for different activities to maximize efficiencies. Similarly, large schools use bells or some other widely broadcast sound to mark the moment when actions begin and end. In a large school with thousands of students and scores of classes, efficient operations depend on everyone adhering to a single uniform schedule; a class can start only when the bell rings and must end when the next bell rings. The system protects instruction—every class will start on time—at the same time that it compromises it—classes must end on time, like work shifts. In other words, while it may be important that every tenth-grade student has a guaranteed number of minutes in world history each day, this guarantee requires that the world history teacher package his or her concepts and instruction in fifty-minute chunks, beginning and ending at a fixed time. Class periods in large high schools are usually between forty-five and fifty-five minutes each, and these time constraints limit what teachers can do. It becomes impossible for a class to dive deeply into a discussion or to be invested or intensely involved in a complex group project when there are inflexible and relatively short increments of time allotted for each subject each day.

In addition to bells, large schools broadcast instructions and announcements using a public address system with speakers (and sometimes closed-circuit televisions) in every classroom. In some schools, announcements over the PA system interrupt classes throughout the day to page students or adults, and although it helps the administrative office to be more efficient, it certainly doesn't assist classroom instruction. As they did in large factories, these tools make no distinction for individual students or teachers—a teacher or student may be in mid-sentence when the bell rings, and an announcement may affect only a single person. Because of the sheer number of people in the organization, however, there is no more efficient and practicable method of communication. The irony is that not only are most contemporary workplaces not factories, but even factories have changed so significantly that few continue to signal work period increments and to convey information by these impersonal methods. Yet these sounds and their purposes persist in most large schools.

Other methods of communication in large schools are similarly designed for mass dissemination and make little distinction among their populations. When students are absent, many large schools use computer-managed prerecorded phone messages to automatically call each absent student's home number to notify the parent (or a voice mail) that the student is not at school and request that a parent verify and explain the absence. The efficiencies of using such an automated system are obvious: even the highest-performing schools average an attendance rate of around 95 percent, and in a large school with at least 1,500 students, it would be considered too time consuming and wasteful to make individual phone calls to the 5 percent, or 75 students' families, every day.

Unfortunately, when a large school does try to personalize and individualize its communication, it often can only do so halfheartedly. In order for back-to-school nights and open house nights to function smoothly, teachers are directed specifically not to have conversations with parents about their individual students. When a large school attempts parent-teacher conferences, they often have the feel of an assembly line, with lines of parents waiting to meet a teacher, and teachers allowed only a few minutes per parent to discuss a child's progress. Efficient, but not very informative. Ironically, even though schools encourage parents and families to attend these conferences, the smooth functioning of parent-teacher conferences depends on not every family attending. The evening of the parent-teacher conference would stretch into the morning if every parent came and if every teacher were to meet, even briefly, with every student's parents. With the prospect of only a few minutes with each teacher, it is not surprising that many parents choose not to make the trip.

Faced with the large numbers of students and families, the school chooses communication systems that facilitate efficient operations but create an impersonal learning environment.

Student Groupings

Because the ultimate goal of most high schools is to have students graduate, large schools organize efficiencies to promote students moving smoothly through their four years. They do this using several different kinds of sorting and grouping, much as large schools did a century ago.

Many large schools, primarily concerned with how many units the student has and how far she is from having the credits to graduate, classify a student's grade level by the number of credits she has accumulated. Rather than determine grade level by academic competency (a student is a tenth grader because she can demonstrate she knows and can do certain skills and content), a student's grade level is a measure of her distance from graduating (a student is a tenth grader because she needs only sixty more credits to graduate).

Grouping students by grade level is only one way large schools organize their students to facilitate smooth paths to graduation. A much more powerful organizing strategy by which large schools organize students to facilitate smooth paths to graduation, and one that has significant repercussions for teaching, learning, and student achievement, is the division of students into academic levels, or "tracks." When the comprehensive high school enrolls a student, she is assigned to an academic track based on a set of data—usually prior test scores, grades, sometimes a placement exam administered by the school, and perhaps prior teachers' input. Students with similar academic scores and prior achievement are placed in the same track, and the courses they take are ostensibly targeted to their academic level. The efficiencies of tracking (whether perceived or actual) are powerful enough to preserve this practice in nearly every large high school in the country despite research-based doubts about its effectiveness and ethical concerns about its inequities.

Let's look more closely at why large schools find tracking so appealing. First, grouping students in classes by similar skill level is believed to make teachers' jobs easier; a teacher can more easily meet students' needs when their needs are similar. When teachers can specialize and their jobs are made easier, the belief goes, less money is required to compensate them, less professional development, and teacher support are required, and fewer material resources are necessary. Just like the arguments supporting nineteenth-century factory design, organizations are thought to be more efficient when their employees can specialize.

Tracking provides other benefits to the school's organization beyond the individual classroom resources and teacher preparation. Tracking enables more efficient allocation and monitoring of classroom resources; rather than providing multiple reading levels of textbooks to every heterogeneously mixed English course, the school can allocate an entire class set of a textbook to the tracked class. Tracking also allows the school to offer a single course at several levels of difficulty, thereby enabling each student to fulfill graduation requirements at the most efficient rate. For example, a student in a low-track biology class and a student in a high-track biology class will each have completed their schoolwide biology requirement for graduation. Finally, and not to be underemphasized, tracking appeases parents of high-achieving students who believe that detracking would compromise their children's education.

But the use of tracking to maximize efficiencies and employee specialization has several costs, powerfully described in Jeannie Oakes's *Keeping Track: How Schools Structure Inequality* (1985). (See Resource A for a summary.)

First, the tracking process is "blunt." A student in a track often takes all courses at that track's academic level even though the student may have different skill competency in different subjects. Usually a student will be placed into the track level that corresponds to the academic level of the subject in which the student is weakest; the student who is strong in language arts but weak in mathematics will likely be placed in a track in which all of her courses, including language arts, will be at a low level. While it may be the simplest and most efficient strategy for assigning classes, tracking does not take into account individual student differences.

Second, *students enter tracking through one-way doors.* Tracking is also a rigid mechanism that doesn't generally allow students to move in and out of tracks as their needs change (Oakes 1985, 51). As entering ninth graders, students are placed into a track based on test scores, grades, and/or teacher recommendations, and they rarely leave that track throughout their high school career. Some students who begin struggling in math may suddenly blossom and become highly interested and competent, but rather than be moved into more challenging tracks, they will simply receive high grades in the low track in which they were initially placed. Similarly, once students are in honors tracks, it is unlikely that they will ever leave that track, which partially explains the pressure on schools and districts to initiate honors tracks as early as possible in the K–12 sequence. Once you're in, you're in.

The most profound and well-documented negative effects of tracking result from the school's differing expectations for each track's students—expectations that are communicated directly and indirectly through adult behavior. Because both teachers and students are aware of and often reinforce these expectations, being in a particular track can have profound effects on the type and quality of instruction students receive as well as their readiness for postgraduation options.

Significant research has shown that teachers' expectations will drive how they teach. Because of the mistaken belief that students with weaker skills are not able to engage in higher-order thinking, tracks for lower-achieving students rely on teacher-centered instruction, rote skills, and less engaging curriculum (strategies that are in fact least likely to help students succeed), while tracks for high-achieving students emphasize student-centered active learning, complex and critical thinking skills, and more engaging activities (strategies that are most likely to help students succeed regardless of achievement level) (Oakes 1985, 110). In addition, because many teachers prefer to teach higher academic tracks and administrations award

Focus point

those classes based on teacher seniority, students in lower tracks often receive the most inexperienced and least qualified faculty.

In contrast to the argument often waged by parents, and sometimes teachers, of high-achieving students, there is overwhelming evidence that tracking does little to aid high-achieving students while it significantly harms students in low tracks (e.g., Oakes 1985, 8) and fragments the school community (Sapon-Shevin 1994). Moreover, because students of color and those from low-income families have been found in disproportionately large percentages in low academic tracks (Oakes 1985, 67), this sorting mechanism raises serious equity concerns. Nevertheless, despite all of the deleterious consequences for student achievement, many schools, especially if they have large numbers of students, continue to track and to identify students by their track because they yield greater efficiencies for getting students through to graduation.

Oakes concludes her text with a number of thought-provoking questions. The most relevant to our discussion is the following: in light of the powerful evidence of tracking's significant harm to the majority of students and limited benefits for the few in the upper track, is simplifying the teaching task—and therefore making the system more efficient—reason enough to justify the practice?

Student Choices and Opportunities

Although large-school structures can limit students, they can also provide an incredible variety of opportunities.

Large high schools are "comprehensive"; they offer a comprehensive set of opportunities to students: sports, arts and music programs, vocational classes, a wide array of electives, after-school programs, and extracurricular activities and clubs. The school can also provide services for many different populations—English learners, special education students, young parents, and students with physical disabilities. Large schools can offer all of these opportunities because a larger school population translates into more resources, even in lower-income communities. Because state and district funding flows to schools based on their student enrollment and attendance, schools with large student populations can often afford large and state-of-the-art facilities, more expensive (and therefore highly experienced) teachers, and high-quality tools for learning. More students usually means more parents, and in large schools this translates into the opportunity to mobilize a larger parent and family community for volunteer support and fundraising. As a supplier of summer and after-school labor for local business, and with many alumni in the community, large schools can access extensive networks to provide supplemental learning experiences to students.

With all of these varied choices, large schools can resemble shopping malls, or even mini-cities, offering health services, food courts, student stores, historical archives, libraries, auditoriums, recreation facilities, and outdoor plazas and central hubs at which to congregate. The concept of the large-school design is that offering so many options increases the likelihood that every student can find curriculum and activities that engage her, no student will be lost with so many possibilities to connect to the school, and every student will find direction with so many options (Powell et al. 1985).

Here we encounter a tension in large schools: the school design is intended to make sure students move toward graduation efficiently, but at the same time the school offers lots of choices and options that would seem to be organizationally cumbersome. Although every choice a large school offers adds complexities to its scheduling, and in doing so compromises the school's efficiencies, by maximizing the number of opportunities the school can keep students enrolled and attending, not just for revenue, but also so that those students pass classes and graduate. As Powell, Farrar, and Cohen explain in

The Shopping Mall High School, "High schools offer accommodations to maximize holding power, graduation
percentages, and customer satisfaction" (1985, 1). In fact,
many large schools expand the number of electives instead of devoting those resources to increasing the number of higher-level classes in the core curriculum (Monk
and Haller 1993, 15).

Yet even with all of these electives to attract students
and "hold" them at the school, it is the student's responsibility to take advantage of these opportunities, a dynamic
that has important postsecondary consequences. In many
large schools, it is up to the student and her family to select the electives and course sequences that meet her interests, needs, and aspirations. Making appropriate choices
amid so many options depends on an informed and sophisticated understanding of the high school and college
admission process—an understanding that most parents
don't have, particularly if they speak limited English or
have limited high school or college experience.

It is true that the student is not entirely without assistance. The school's guidance counselors are intended to
help students and families select appropriate courses and
navigate the high school experience. Yet in most large
schools, hundreds of students are assigned to each counselor, making meaningful individualized counseling nearly
impossible. Guidance counselors can't know their students well and aren't able to help each one organize an
academic plan that strengthens her development and positions her for college admission. So not every student gets
sufficient attention. Guidance counselors are particularly
critical to ensure equitable access to postsecondary opportunities for those students who come from families with
limited experience with the college admission or financing
processes—generally low-income students and English
learners—but it is in schools with high numbers of these
students where the counselor shortage is most acute.

According to the National Association for College Admission Counseling, the national average of students to

college counselors in high schools that serve over 2,000 students is 515:1, while for schools that enroll between 500 and 999 students, the ratio is 328:1, nearly 200 fewer students per college counselor (Clinedinst 2008). Other reports show that in large urban areas the overall average ratio is 740:1 (Fitzsimmons 1991). Under these large student loads, guidance counselors can act only as registrars and transcript reviewers, simply confirming that each student is taking the correct sequence of required courses in the correct tracks for a timely graduation. It is in this capacity that they can best facilitate the school's efficiencies.

Teachers' Work Contexts

Because the teacher's experience in a small school will be described in detail in subsequent chapters, a discussion of the teacher's work environment in a typical large school provides an important point of reference.

Teachers' experiences are significantly affected by their "student load"—the number of students seen in one day's classes—and teachers in large schools generally have large student loads (a conservative estimate is a class size of 30, multiplied by five different classes of students, for a total of 150 students per day), which has several consequences for teacher practice. It doesn't only mean 150 names to remember. Every time a teacher assigns work to students, that work must be graded—and the thought of grading 150 assignments is a powerful disincentive against giving complex assignments that call for deeper thinking and more expansive student responses. Instead, it is more sensible to create assignments that are easy to grade, such as multiple-choice responses and fill-in-the-blanks. This lesson I learned the hard way during my first year of teaching in Atlanta.

Time spent grading papers is time taken away from curriculum planning, so grading large numbers of assignments also results in less time for teachers to construct lessons that flow from their own priorities and instructional preferences. With so many students it becomes more difficult to diagnose students' skill weaknesses and identify their learning styles. Along with having less time available because of more papers to grade, *teachers with large student loads have every reason to choose a one-size-fits-all "packaged" curriculum—to progress sequentially through the textbook and use the book's questions for student assignments—and teacher-centered instructional strategies such as lecturing instead of creating curriculum and instruction that adjust to and accommodate their students' different needs.*

Focus point

These combined dynamics can drive many teachers to create traditional classrooms, if only because using those strategies helps them to survive such large student loads. This also may explain why teachers in large high schools are prized for being entertaining: within a traditional teacher-centered pedagogy, teachers increase their effectiveness with an engaging teacher-centered style; they can't practicably afford to increase their effectiveness by developing differentiated or student-centered lessons.

In terms of professional growth opportunities, large schools offer plenty of colleagues to provide assistance and share resources. Teachers in high school are content area specialists—assigned to a department and rarely teaching outside that subject area. Because of this specialization, multiple teachers in each department can offer peer assistance about that content area—a benefit particularly to a new teacher. Unfortunately, department meetings are often entirely administrative (scheduling finals or ordering supplies) and rarely provide an environment to learn from fellow professionals. Instead, teachers in large schools typically must seek assistance on their own, building informal networks with colleagues.

Just as student differentiation is subordinated to efficiency, so it is for teachers' learning experiences. Although every teacher has her own needs and strengths and is at a unique point in the development of her practice, the professional development (by that I mean structured forums intended for teacher learning) in most large schools is generally provided through agencies external to the school. Usually, it is the district office or third-party organizations that present a one-size-fits-all workshop that has little relationship to the specific context of each teacher's practice—her students or her development as a teacher. Additionally, because there is scant opportunity for teachers to watch each other teach in large schools, even the discussions within departments rarely address the specific context of each teacher's classroom.

Paradoxically, even as they are surrounded by large numbers of peers, teachers in large high schools may have difficulty building collaborative relationships with colleagues. Teachers in large schools can behave as scores of "independent contractors," each teaching her classes privately behind her closed door. The anonymity, isolation, and depersonalization that can occur with students in many large high schools can be experienced by teachers as well.

As we can see from the four characteristics discussed in this chapter, large high schools are designed to maximize graduation rates through efficient systems and specialization. They typically do this through student groupings, mass communication tools, and a wide variety of curricular and extracurricular options. The large-school structure encourages teachers to use simplified assessment, traditional curriculum, and teacher-centered pedagogy. Teachers specialize in their subject area and focus on their classroom, and they have few opportunities to work meaningfully with colleagues, especially outside their department. Both students and teachers may have varied opportunities available to grow and learn, but it is up to them to navigate the system and find the resources that best fit them.

These are some of the "bells" institutionalized in the large high school. Many students in comprehensive high schools, because of the dedication of their teachers or because of the educational resources they bring to the

Paradoxically, even as they are surrounded by large numbers of peers, teachers in large high schools may have difficulty building collaborative relationships with colleagues.

school (family, home environment, and previous schooling), are successful in this learning environment. We will learn later how some exemplary teachers in large high schools are able to essentially overcome the institutional restrictions of their school to serve their students. But for an unacceptable and, frankly, unconscionable number of students, the large high school has failed to meet their needs and the needs of our modern society. As Andy Hargreaves characterizes secondary schools: "Their large, complex, bureaucratic structures are ill suited to the dynamic and varying needs of the postmodern world: needs for more relevant and engaging student learning, for more continuous and connected professional development, and for more flexible and inclusive decision-making" (1994, 28). Small schools set out to meet these needs, for students and their teachers.

IMPORTANT CHARACTERISTICS OF SMALL HIGH SCHOOLS

Schools with small numbers of students generally do not prioritize educational efficiency. Instead, staff in small schools often believe that the relationships among the students and teachers are the most important feature of a school—that students learn better when they are connected to their teachers and each other in meaningful ways. While the following chapters will examine the small school in greater detail, here I will touch on the most significant characteristics of small schools that distinguish them from large schools.

Communication Methods

Compared with the large school, communication in the small school can be more intimate and personalized. When a message needs to be communicated to all students, rather than using a public address system to share information, many small schools' staff and students gather weekly, or even daily, to build school community together. When it comes to communication between two individuals, while in a large school it can be difficult to find, let alone talk with, a specific student or colleague, a small school—because it has a smaller facility with fewer people—requires less effort to locate and contact another member of the school. The logistics of communication become simpler, making it more likely for people to co-ordinate, share information, and listen to each other. In fact, for reasons that will be explained in more detail in Chapter 4, the ease of communication in small schools makes the systems and structures of the school more malleable. LaRavian Battle explains:

> Suppose I had students in my third-period class, and fourth period I had a prep period, so I had some free time. I could go and pull them out of their next fourth-period class for maybe ten minutes. I didn't want to take up all their next period, but just a few minutes to clarify some things with them that maybe they didn't get quite right on a quiz. Because it's a small school I have that ability to talk with my colleagues: "You know, so-and-so is really having trouble with this concept. Can I pull them out for this?" And most of the time they would say yes, and I would do the same thing for them, of course.

LaRavian dismissed students but then, with the next teacher's permission, essentially extended the class for a few students. The flexibility of the small-school struc-ture, and the opportunity for teachers to mutually agree to alter those structures, flow from this ease of commu-nication as well as the relationships the communication facilitates.

In small schools, bells are as unnecessary as PA an-nouncements. With fewer staff and students, teachers can arrange different class schedules within the same school. Even when all teachers need to follow the same schedule, the small number of faculty makes them mutually responsible to each other to follow the schedule, so they don't need the bells. It also becomes less important that they all end instruction at the same instant; not having bells allows teachers the flexibility to finish conversations and ideas before they dismiss students. Chapters 2 through 4 will explore more deeply all of these interrelated dynamics—accessibility, mutual accountability, and shared agreements.

Student Groupings

Small schools rarely track students, in part because it is logistically unfeasible. For example, if there are only 100 students in the ninth grade (not an unusual number of students in a small high school) and, according to a reading test, 11 students demonstrate significant reading deficits, 30 students are below grade level, 41 are on grade level, and 18 show they are ready for additional challenges, the distribution doesn't lend itself to tracking those students into 35-student classes. Furthermore, some small schools reject tracking because knowing students as individuals makes it harder for the adults to classify students merely by their score on a particular test, their grades in a series of courses, or their performance in a particular setting. They know that their students' strengths and needs are more complex and less easily categorized into academic tracks. Moreover, knowing them well often makes teachers unwilling to consign some students to lower expectations than others.

Focus point

A large school enables teachers to have varied expectations about what and how students should learn (the many levels of ninth-grade English with assorted quality of assignments, for example) but relatively narrow expectations about how students learn (undifferentiated, with easy-to-grade assignments and teacher-centered pedagogy). By contrast, small schools can have narrow expectations for what students can learn (all students will be qualified for entrance to college) but varied expectations for how they learn (complex and individualized pedagogical approaches) because they know their students so well.

Student Choices and Opportunities

One limitation of small schools is that they cannot offer the same range of resources and opportunities as large schools. The choices of clubs, sports, and electives are limited in small schools because of the cost of supporting activities (less money because of fewer students) and their dependence on faculty sponsors (fewer adults means fewer sponsors). Additionally, for an activity to be offered, a critical mass of students must be interested in it, but with fewer students it is harder in the small school to amass enough students with that interest to warrant investing resources. Small schools rarely have football teams or marching bands: these activities call for significant funding (uniforms, equipment, transportation, facility space), need multiple faculty sponsors, and require large numbers of students, all of which small schools lack. As compared with a large school, where extracurriculars are a major focus of the school, in small schools the extracurricular activities are more peripheral to school life.

Interestingly, research has found that although small schools may have fewer extracurricular activities, the rate of student participation in the activities is actually *higher* than in large schools (Cotton 1996; Leithwood and Jantzi 2009). When students feel more connected to the school and the people there, they are more interested in participating in after-school activities, independent of what those activities are. Robert Crosnoe and his coauthors found that "each increase in school size was associated with a decrease in the predicted extracurricular participation" (2004, 1270). And while at a large school dozens of students, even hundreds, may be competing for the starting positions on a team, in small schools there is less competition for spots, and after-school activities become more available and accessible to all students. (See also Barker and Gump 1964; Cotton 1996; Gladden 1998; Leithwood and Jantzi 2009.)

**Relationships
are not a by-
product of the
small school;
they are the
*intentional
dynamic of
teaching and
learning.***

Teachers' Work Context

This crucial aspect of small schools is the primary focus of this book. Fewer teachers means colleagues can have more meaningful and productive relationships. Teachers can work collaboratively with colleagues in ways impossible in large schools and, in doing so, can have a profound impact on students' learning experiences across classrooms and even outside the classroom. Teachers in small schools also have the opportunity, and obligation, to contribute to the larger decisions of the school and to be part of a cohesive and interdependent community of teachers and learners. But these opportunities are not guaranteed just because the school is small, nor, as we will see, are they without costs.

The small high school is not just a large high school with fewer students. Instead, having fewer students provides a different context in which teachers can explore opportunities for teaching and learning. It seems obvious that with fewer students, students and teachers would get to know each other. But these relationships are not a by-product of the small school; they are the *intentional dynamic of teaching and learning.* A premise of small schools is that it is only by knowing students as individuals—their strengths, weaknesses, interests, learning styles, and circumstances—that teachers can provide appropriate instruction.

Although it may seem that my characterization of large and small high schools is binary—one doesn't have relationships, and the other does—I don't believe that teachers in large schools can't, or don't, connect with students to improve student learning. In this book we will hear from teachers who have. Some graduates from large high schools had a connection with a teacher that was important to their high school experience; that relationship may have inspired some of us to be teachers. Small schools, as we will see, have structures and systems to facilitate relationships regardless of the initiative of the teacher or the personality of the student.

CONCLUSION

The organizing principle by which to understand the distinction between large and small high schools is that large schools educate through
maximizing efficiencies, order, and specialization: how can we educate
the most students in the most efficient manner? Small schools, by contrast, generally reflect and encourage a method of educating that priori-
tizes relationships as prerequisites to high achievement: how can we get
to know each student and draw upon that knowledge and relationship
to meet her needs? These two deep foundational and opposing strategies, whether intentional or not, drive nearly every school function and
have profound implications for student and teacher learning.

This chapter has focused primarily on large schools in order to define
the reference point for small schools. The next chapter begins with a
discussion of the pedagogical and philosophical bases for prioritizing relationships in the learning process and then examines the relationships
in small schools between teachers and the students in their classrooms.

DISCUSSION QUESTIONS

1. How does the way your school is organized influence the relationships that arise among teachers, among students, and between teachers and students? In what ways do adults' beliefs
   about teaching, learning, and students affect the likelihood of
   relationships?

2. Think about your own teachers, your colleagues, and yourself.
   To what degree do you think the sizes of the schools you attended and/or work in shape your beliefs about teaching and
   learning? To what degree do you think your beliefs about teaching and learning drove what schools you chose to attend and/or
   work at?

3. How do schools model and reinforce values for students? What
   kind of values are large schools modeling, and reinforcing, in
   students? What about in small schools?

FURTHER READING

Oakes, Jeannie. 1985. *Keeping Track: How Schools Structure Inequality.* New Haven, CT: Yale University Press.

Powell, Arthur G., Eleanor Farrar, and David K. Cohen. 1985. *The Shopping Mall High School: Winners and Losers in the Educational Marketplace.* Boston: Houghton Mifflin.

Tyack, David B. 1974. *The One Best System: A History of American Urban Education.* Cambridge, MA: Harvard University Press.

CHAPTER TWO

THE TEACHER'S EXPERIENCE IN A SMALL SCHOOL

Relationships with Students

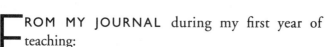

FROM MY JOURNAL during my first year of teaching:

In my ninth period English class today, Kindra, who struggles a lot with reading, was about to put her head down as we were watching a video, and I wrote her a note that said that I know she can be successful and that I would be willing to tutor her after school with English or any other subject. She read it, folded it, and put it in her book. I asked her at the end of class if she was interested, and she said she'd have to check with her mom. I hope something works out with this, because she is ripe to slip through every one of the school's cracks: she's not very motivated, is tardy to class, has some attitude, and doesn't respond well to teachers who don't challenge her, and frankly, doesn't respond that well to teachers who do challenge her.

I'm not sure why I'm trying to connect and help Kindra; there are other students in a similar situation.
Shouldn't I be giving notes to all of the students and
making the same offer? But I don't think this strategy
would work with every student—I just think I know her
enough to try this. Why do I think I've figured out how
to connect with Kindra but not with other students?

As we saw in the last chapter, large high schools historically have emphasized standardization, specialization, and
efficiencies, and have "processed pupils in batches . . .
taught them a standardized course or curriculum, and did
this through teacher-centered methods of lecturing, recitation, question-and-answer and seatwork" (Hargreaves
1994, 27). Opposed to this paradigm is valuing the relationship between a teacher and her students—which I now
specifically define as *the teacher's knowledge of her students
and, because of this knowledge, how she teaches*—as a key part
of the learning process. Although small schools prioritize
relationships among all members of the school community,
in this chapter I will focus on the classroom relationships:
how does the teacher in a small school know her students,
and how do those relationships affect teaching and learning? As we will see, having fewer students in a school profoundly affects a teacher's classroom experience when that
smaller population results in fewer students per class or
fewer students in a teacher's student load—or even when
there is no reduction in either class size or student load.

Before I discuss the dynamics and implications of
these relationships, it is important to identify some key
figures whose work supports the belief that student
learning depends on relationships.

THE IMPORTANCE OF RELATIONSHIPS FOR TEACHING AND LEARNING: THEORY

The first aspect of my definition of relationships—the
teacher's knowledge of the student—is supported by

John Dewey, who called for a pedagogy in which children's learning depended not on a rationally well-crafted and standardized curriculum but on the teacher knowing and interacting constructively with her students. In *The Child and the Curriculum*, first published in 1902, Dewey applied psychological principles to the classroom and asserted that learning occurs within a situation that is unique to each child's context. Therefore, the teacher's goal is to use the child's past experiences and present interests to "induce a vital and personal experiencing" (Dewey 1956, 201). The teacher should draw on something in the child's background that "has previously occupied a significant position in the child's life for its own sake" (203) to engender in the student a curiosity and intrinsic motivation to learn. *Engaging students by connecting the curriculum to their interests is not just an important way of teaching. To Dewey, it is the only way to have authentic learning; all other attempts to make students learn are false and artificial:*

Focus point

> If the subject-matter of the lessons be such as to have an appropriate place within the expanding consciousness of the child, if it grows out of his own past doings, thinkings, and sufferings, and grows into application in further achievements and receptivities, then no device or trick of method has to be resorted to in order to enlist "interest." . . . But the externally presented material, conceived and generated in standpoints and attitudes remote from the child, and developed in motives alien to him, has no such place of its own. Hence the recourse to adventitious leverage to push it in, to factitious drill to drive it in, to artificial bribe to lure it in. (1956, 205)

Tapping into students' interests is a more powerful way to engage students than extrinsic motivation of carrots (honor roll, high grades, graduation) or sticks (low grades, retention). For example, if the teacher wants the student to learn to write a persuasive essay, the topic of the essay should come from the student's individual background and beliefs, and that ownership of the ideas will motivate the student to learn to express her ideas effectively.

Interestingly, research has found that engaging students' interests does not just create motivation to learn but correlates with deeper levels of cognition, comprehension, and concentration (Schiefele and Csikszentmihalyi 1994, 1995). As Ulrich Schiefele writes, quoting Mihaly Csikszentmihalyi, "The chief problem is not a lack of ability, but of motivation. Consequently, educators should focus on the intrinsic rewards of the various subject areas and bear in mind that, if 'intrigued by the opportunities of the domain, most students will make sure to develop the skills they need to operate within it'" (Schiefele 1991, 318). Interest motivates students to learn, but it also facilitates them learning more deeply. If the persuasive essay is not just an exercise for a grade but has a relevant audience, with an opportunity for the students' words to make a difference, the students will want to make the most sophisticated argument with the highest-quality rhetorical strategies regardless of the teacher's rewards or punishments.

Though not stated explicitly by Dewey or Schiefele, motivating a student by connecting curriculum to her interests depends on a sophisticated understanding of the student. Only when the teacher knows each student well enough to identify the student's key prior experiences and interests, and then uses that information to facilitate current learning, can the teacher engender in the student the motivation to learn through relevant content as well as the opportunity to learn through appropriately tailored instruction.

This is the second aspect of the learning relationship: the quality of the interaction between the student and teacher in the learning process. Vygotsky, a developmental psychologist, asserted that there are skills a student can do independently (her "developmental level"), other skills that are entirely beyond a student's reach, and somewhere in between a range of skills that a student can do with assistance. This range of skills Vygotsky called the "zone of proximal development": "What is the zone of proximal development today will be the actual developmental level tomorrow—that is, what a child can do with assistance today she will be able to do by herself tomorrow" (1978, 87).

An example of this is a student's reading level. There is a level at which the student can read independently, and there are reading levels entirely beyond her current skills, but in between there is a range of texts she can read with assistance. This assistance can take the form of prereading discussions related to the content or vocabulary, guiding questions during the reading, or other literacy and comprehension strategies. With assistance within her zone of proximal development, the student will eventually be able to read the text independently that she had previously been able to read only with assistance, and her zone of proximal development for reading shifts upward.

Interestingly, Vygotsky thought that learning doesn't occur within the zone of proximal development; learning helps to *create* the zone of proximal development: "Learning awakens a variety of internal developmental processes that are able to operate only when the child is interacting with people in his environment and in cooperation with his peers. Once these processes are internalized, they become part of the child's independent developmental achievement" (1978, 90). In this model of learning, the student's intellectual growth depends on the teacher not to provide information but to guide and facilitate the student's encounter with a task individually appropriate to the student, and to position the student's peers as important collaborators. The teacher's understanding of the student is key to student learning; when I know my students well enough to identify their zones of proximal development, I can identify appropriate instructional material and foster engaging and suitable interactions.

This pedagogy is in direct contrast to the mode of teaching in which the teacher provides a one-size-fits-all curriculum and expects that students will motivate themselves to invest the effort to complete the assigned tasks. Instead, drawing on the theories of both Vygotsky and Dewey, we can conclude that students learn because (1) a teacher has a relationship with them; (2) she knows them well enough to identify their needs and next stage of learning; and (3) she motivates them by tapping into their interests and experiences. In this paradigm, the teacher's role is to know students well enough to create personalized instruction that challenges every student and meets every student's needs. This is the belief behind differentiation and the operating premise of small schools.

THE IMPORTANCE OF RELATIONSHIPS FOR TEACHING AND LEARNING: PRACTICE

> MICHAEL: Relationships are a form of currency, and if you're going to be asking young people in their adolescent resistance to do certain things, having that relationship helps a long way to be allies rather than to be on different sides of the table.

Cross-Reference See Book 4, Chapter I for a discussion of teacher-student relationships.

Along with factors such as greater safety and a strong sense of accountability between schools and families, Wasley and her coauthors identify "a greater variety in instructional approaches" (2000, 33) as a key reason for the successes of the Chicago small schools they studied. A "more varied instructional repertoire for working with students" is also identified among the reasons the teachers in small schools felt a greater sense of self-efficacy than those in large schools (Cotton 2001, 37). What is the connection between these learning theories and the engaging and differentiated instructional techniques that research has identified in successful small schools? Let's start by understanding what differentiation entails and requires from teachers.

Key concept *Differentiation*

Differentiation, tailoring curriculum and instruction based on student differences so every student has equal opportunities to succeed, has become an expectation of teachers everywhere, regardless of school environment, size, or structure. According to Carol Ann Tomlinson, teachers can differentiate in three ways. First, the teacher can adjust curriculum and instruction according to students' differing skill levels, or "readiness" (for example, by using different texts for different reading proficiencies). The teacher can also accommodate students' different learning styles (by providing information visually and verbally, having students work in groups or alone, and so forth). Finally, the teacher can appeal to different students' interests (by connecting fractions to a student's interest in music) (Tomlinson 1999, 11). Differentiation expresses the practical application of Dewey and Vygotsky: students need to be genuinely engaged in their learning, and teachers need to create learning tasks that build on what the student can already do and are within each student's reach with some assistance. More recently, differentiation has included cultural responsiveness— creating learning opportunities that recognize and use students' cultural experiences and values (see, e.g., Banks 2004; Gay 2000; and Ladson-Billings 1994).

Educators generally recognize the value of differentiation, espoused in schools' goals and professional development plans. Unfortunately, pledges of differentiated strategies in classrooms are often "more honored in the breach than the observance" (*Hamlet*, Act I, scene 4). The problem is that successful differentiation depends upon each teacher knowing her students well enough to identify their strengths, needs, interests, learning styles, and backgrounds. If you don't know each student that well, how do you know what or how to differentiate? As Peter Ross, director of LEADS Network at Stanford University, says, "Teachers need to differentiate instruction in any school, but it's far easier to tailor instruction to the individual needs of particular students in a small school because the teachers know them so much better than they do in a large school. [In a large school] you might

TEXTBOX 2.1   CULTURALLY RESPONSIVE TEACHING

First identified by Gloria Ladson-Billings, culturally responsive (or relevant) teaching is a "pedagogy that empowers students intellectually, socially, emotionally, and politically by using cultural referents to impart knowledge, skills, and attitudes" (Ladson-Billings 1994, 17–18). In her book *Culturally Responsive Teaching* (2000), Geneva Gay identified some key aspects of this kind of teaching:

- validates students' prior experiences, cultural knowledge, and performance styles;
- comprehensively develops academic success, cultural competence, and critical social consciousness;
- is multidimensional, encompassing curriculum content, learning context, classroom climate, student-teacher relationships, instructional techniques, and performance assessments;
- empowers students to become better human beings and more successful learners by engendering academic competence, personal confidence, courage, and the will to act;
- is transformative, defying conventions of traditional educational practices with respect to students of color;
- is emancipatory, making authentic knowledge about different ethnic groups accessible to students, liberating them from the constraints of mainstream canons of knowledge and ways of knowing.

identify a particular learning target and be successful with that, but you might not be able to come up with a really deep plan for that student to move them." Teachers who serve large numbers of students often find it nearly impossible to differentiate because they aren't able to know their students as individuals. As a result, teachers in large schools may be trained to differentiate but can't fully exploit the theory and its related strategies. In a large school, a teacher might know that a student has trouble reading and give the student a book at a lower reading level. But the teacher isn't able to know the student well enough to identify the source of the student's reading difficulties and therefore can't develop a more targeted plan to address her needs. Small schools, by definition and often through internal structures, promote ways for teachers to know students well so that teaching and learning become differentiated.

A teacher's knowledge of her students informs her practice in several ways. First, knowledge of a student's contexts and personality—"the whole student"—can generate understanding for a student who struggles or exhibits unproductive behaviors. The teacher recognizes that each student has good and bad days, pressures and supports, and plenty of interests and talents that affect what he does in the classroom. Knowing a student also means learning about a student's family, home, and neighborhood environments—all of which are outside the classroom but which can significantly affect the student within the classroom. As a result of knowing about a student's personality, history, and context, a teacher can adjust and target his strategies to engage that student. Stacie Pierpoint, a Spanish teacher in a small school in Washington, DC, gives an example:

> I had one girl in my classroom who had never learned single-digit multiplication, and she had a lot of behavior problems in my classrooms and other classrooms. Over time and through talking and building a relationship, [I learned that] a lot of behavior issues were related to the fact that she was embarrassed about being so far behind the other students. And once I knew that, I could work with her and figure out ways to meet her where she was and get her where the other students are.

Second, as teachers develop relationships with students and understand them, they gain information to diagnose each student's specific skill and content gaps, the learning styles to capitalize on, and the student's interests and strengths, and with this information, they can provide higher-quality instruction individually tailored to each student.

Stacie Pierpoint and LaRavian Battle talk about how knowing students well in their small schools enabled them to personalize instruction:

> STACIE PIERPOINT: I had a ninth-grade student who, every time we did anything that involved using markers or pencils, orange and green were always on his desk because they were the color of his favorite sport team. I discovered that correcting his papers in those colors actually made him focus on the corrections I made. If I did things that used color, like putting things on flash cards, I actually made an extra effort to put things in those colors for him specifically. It had been really hard to motivate him or figure out how to get him to participate in class. He didn't really want to do the work, but I started getting more of a return in the work he was completing after I started noticing that he liked those colors. He had more investment and interest in class.
>
> LaRAVIAN: I had one ninth grader who had had really bad experiences in math and didn't feel confident at all. She would give up on quizzes and not finish anything because she just didn't feel like she could. I noticed that whenever I would release them to go and start doing their work and help each other, she wanted to explain the strategies again to me, to vocalize them for herself. I realized that she needed to talk about the work in order to really understand, and so I put her in groups with other students that needed to hear it so she could speak about it more. Her grades went up tremendously.

In both of these cases, knowing students equipped teachers well with the information they needed to differentiate their instruction and facilitate student success. Both teachers "discovered," "noticed," and "realized" something specific about their students that they could use to provide more effective instruction. The changes they made seem simple—using specific colors or allowing a student to verbalize knowledge to others—but this information would have been invisible were it not for the teachers being able to have relationships with their students and learn about them.

Third, a more informed understanding of students not only yields a more nuanced, caring, and strategic approach to teaching and learning interactions with them but can also engender in teachers a stronger investment in their students' success. It's much easier to ignore struggling or disobedient students if you don't know them, their lives, or their specific needs and gifts. But when a teacher knows and understands her students, it is harder for her to write off a student who struggles or to attribute a student's low performance to an assumed lack of motivation. The teacher recognizes that a student's fragile home environment may be contributing to her difficulty completing homework or that a student's misbehavior is how she distracts others from noticing her weak math skills. In Stacie's case, knowing that her student's behavior was a manifestation of a lack of confidence in academic skills enabled her to strategically create learning supports (scaffolding and targeted preteaching) to facilitate her student's growth and self-esteem through skill competency. The teacher who has developed personalized relationships with students—knowing each of them well as learners and as people—sees them as young people who all want to succeed but who have very different circumstances, talents, and hurdles with which to strive for that success. This perspective allows the teacher to create personalized and differentiated learning experiences.

When a teacher doesn't get the opportunity to know her students, the explanation for students' struggles remains a mystery, which can cause the teacher to make assumptions that she lacks the expertise to help the student or, worse, that the student lacks the ability or desire to succeed. By contrast, knowing more about a student can actually engender optimistic beliefs and aspirational expectations about the student's capacity for success and be more committed to and responsible for facilitating that success.

> LaRavian: I feel a lot more connected to my students—how they score on the benchmarks or their grades. I just feel a lot more connected to students and their families and feel as if it's my responsibility. I'm analyzing standards and looking through spreadsheets and looking at trends in my class data. I feel like the responsibility for those grades is much, much more mine than in the past [when I taught at a large school]. If there was a student who had a problem in my class, we'd just give a referral and say, "Go away. You're somebody else's problem." I don't feel as if I can do that as much here [in a small school], because they're my students. I know these kids better, I feel more connected to these students and invested in them achieving, to meet[ing] students where they're at and bringing them forward.

These three effects of knowing your students—the understanding of their individual contexts, the informed identification of their learning needs and strengths, and the emotional and moral responsibility you feel to not allow students to fail—are what make relationships so powerful for teaching and learning. In both large and small schools, LaRavian had students for which she was responsible, but it was not until she taught in a small school that she truly owned that responsibility, the disposition that the students were "my students."

One final result of relationships is that when students are known and a teacher uses that knowledge to help them succeed, they trust that teacher. Students who trust their teachers feel more comfortable reaching out for academic support as well as for help with relationships, peer pressure, and family conflicts and needs. Stacie recognized that when students are more comfortable asking for assistance, they actually build self-advocacy skills:

> At our school our students didn't have a lot of experiences with adults that are very positive, and I think that being able to ask for help is connected to trust: is this person going to make fun of me, or is this person going to judge me because I don't know what I should or because I am having this problem at home? [When I was student teaching in a large school,] I may have had two or three kids really seek out help from either the teacher I was working for or myself. But in a smaller school, because they're building relationships long-term with teachers, they cannot feel stupid for asking for help. They have this bond that allows them to take care of themselves a little better and advocate for themselves. Relationships are important, as far as learning to trust other people in order to get what you need.

The teacher who says, "I have office hours after school; the students who need it just don't come," hasn't yet realized that students must trust their teachers enough to feel safe disclosing their needs and asking for help. This is true especially for those students who struggle—and have always struggled—in school, who have never had positive relationships with their teachers. Students have to trust their teachers in order to take risks in their learning, and this trust is based on their confidence that teachers know them well and will use that knowledge to help them.

As Linda Darling-Hammond explains, "Relationships matter for learning. Students' trust in their teachers helps them develop the commitment and motivation needed to tackle challenging learning tasks. Teachers' connections to and understanding of their students help those students develop the commitment and capacity to surmount the hurdles that accompany ambitious learning" (1997, 134).

Cross-Reference **For a discussion on the importance of trust between students and teachers, see Book 5, Chapter 3.**

Most of us, regardless of our school's size or context, recognize the importance of getting to know our students. But we can only hope to establish truly meaningful teaching and learning relationships—to know our students well enough so we can personalize their academic experiences—if institutional structures make it easier for us to know them and limit the number of students we're expected to know. Just as large schools have systems intended to facilitate the efficient processing of students through their four years, many small schools draw upon the theories of Dewey and Vygotsky and organize themselves to promote teacher-student relationships in order to improve student learning. They do this by limiting the number of students in a teacher's class, in a teacher's load, and in the school.

SMALLNESS: CLASS SIZE, STUDENT LOAD, SCHOOL ENROLLMENT

Most teachers intuitively recognize that a key benefit of a *small class size*—limiting the number of students taught at one time in a classroom—is that it is easier to attend to each student during a class period when there are fewer students. Because much of a student's learning occurs within the classroom, with a smaller class size the teacher can get a more complete understanding of how her students are progressing during the instruction and can spend more time with the students who need individualized attention during that class period. Experienced teachers use instructional activities that assess student learning and give the teacher information about how well each student is progressing toward mastering the lesson's skill or content goal. With fewer students, teachers can more easily assess students as well as provide additional support to struggling students based on their assessment.

A teacher's *student load* is the total number of students she serves—the sum of all students in all of her classes. A small student load has a broader effect on a teacher's practice than having a small class size because it affects not only what a teacher does within the class but also how she prepares her curriculum and instruction outside the class period. Like the teacher with a smaller class size, the teacher with a smaller student load has more opportunities to know each student as an individual learner. But in addition, the teacher with fewer total students also has more ways to do something with this knowledge.

The teacher with a large student load often finds herself overwhelmed by stacks of assignments to grade, resulting either in long turnaround times for students to get feedback on their work or less time for the teacher to plan the next day's lesson—both of which weaken the quality of teaching and learning. Certain instructional strategies are much more possible to implement well when student load is lowered. With fewer total students to teach each day, there are fewer assignments to grade and the teacher can afford to spend more time evaluating each student's work, which therefore enables her to assign more complex tasks with more authentic assessments. For example, to teach writing requires the teacher to review student progress throughout the writing process—brainstorming, organizing, and writing multiple drafts. Project-based learning, in which students learn skills and content through open-ended and student-driven investigation and performance, requires the teacher to monitor, coach, support, and evaluate each student individually.

The teacher with a large student load, regardless of her vision or intent, is less willing and able to facilitate this kind of learning because it requires so much time to read and critique the developing work of every student. The teacher with a large student load may have no choice but to assign tasks that can be graded quickly and therefore address more superficial student understanding: using multiple-choice and true/false questions to assess lower-order recall skills rather than measuring students' ability to synthesize information through essay assignments or portfolios, which demand planning, coaching, and time to complete and depend on the teacher knowing students as individuals and helping all of them, each in her own way, to meet expectations.

Reducing student load can have a greater effect on a student's experience than smaller class size, because while smaller class size changes the amount of individualized instructional time the teacher can allocate to each student, a smaller student load changes the broader instructional experience for every student the teacher teaches. Receiving a few more minutes of individual attention each class period in a smaller class is helpful, but more beneficial is having a deeper, more engaging curriculum with higher-quality instruction and more authentic assessments by a teacher who has sufficient time.

Even though it might seem obvious that small classes always translate into small student loads, and vice versa, they don't. Schools can provide their teachers with one aspect of "smallness" without the other. A school can reduce class size but still have teachers teach six classes each day. Conversely, even if schools can't reduce class size, they can reduce student load through block scheduling or integrating subjects so that the teacher sees fewer students for longer amounts of time (see Resource B).

Smaller class sizes change the relationship between the teacher and the individual student during the specific class, and a smaller student load changes the relationship and learning opportunities between the teacher and all of her students. A school with *a smaller total student enrollment* can change the relationships among the teachers and students to promote a personalized learning environment schoolwide.

In a large comprehensive high school, a teacher rarely teaches the same students more than once. Therefore, each school year, and sometimes each semester, the teacher works with an entirely new set of students, with completely different personalities, needs, and interests. In a small high school, fewer students and fewer teachers mean that a teacher is likely to teach the same student two or even three times during four years. This can happen through deliberate "looping" structures, in which teachers teach the same students for multiple years. It can also happen inadvertently; because, as we will learn in more detail later, each teacher in a small school has to teach many different courses, usually including an elective, many students have no choice but to be taught by the same teacher for several courses during their high school years. While some teachers fear looping because of the challenge of learning, planning, and implementing different curricula each year, seeing the same students in multiple courses enables the teacher to draw upon her previous interaction with and understanding of the students to accommodate, and even anticipate, students' needs and strengths more quickly and effectively.

> STACIE PIERPOINT: There were students that I had in the ninth grade that I taught again in the eleventh grade, so having that relationship established already from the ninth grade, they knew me as a teacher. By the time I had them again in the eleventh grade, they already knew what my expectations were, and they had a relationship with me. It helps a lot with instruction. Last year I had two students who really struggled with other teachers who were new to them, but who I didn't have any behavior problems with because I already knew a lot about them. I knew how to teach them from when I had them in the ninth grade.

Stacie's example illustrates how multiyear relationships with students allow teachers to be more effective. The teacher who has students in her class she has taught previously has a much easier time ritualizing and enforcing classroom expectations and structures. The time and energy invested the previous year to build a classroom culture means that the teacher doesn't have to start from scratch; the same students already know the expectations and "how we do things here." The teacher already has a yearlong relationship with each of her students and can capitalize on her deep understanding of them to have more meaningful learning activities earlier in the year. And having worked with the students previously, the teacher can spend less time assessing students' prior knowledge; not only does she already know students' skills, but she knows exactly how students learned many of these skills because she taught them. She becomes more accountable to prepare students for the next year's course if she is the one teaching that course.

Besides the opportunities in small schools to teach students multiple times, and the power of those long-term relationships for student learning, a school with a small total enrollment affects the interactions between teachers and *the students they don't teach.* Even though most administrators expect their teachers to supervise students, either during specific supervision assignments or more generally during passing periods and assemblies, it is difficult for many teachers to relate to students they don't teach or haven't taught in the past.

Safety is a serious concern in large schools because students and teachers are anonymous. When students aren't known, they behave with more impunity toward adults and less concern for the impact of their actions on other students (who are similarly anonymous to them). As Michael Soguero explains, teachers behave differently toward those students they don't know: "One of the problems in big schools is anonymity. There is just a different way that an adult walks up to a young person who they don't recognize. In the large school building that I was in, some of the students who were not known were treated as suspects from the moment that somebody came up to them."

It becomes a frustrating experience for many teachers to negotiate their role in the "common spaces" of school—the hallways, the cafeteria, the auditorium—and during unstructured time when students are not in class—before and after school and between classes. If you don't know the student's name, much less who she is and what she responds to, it's hard to manage her behavior. When students don't know you as a teacher, your only chance of being respected is if the students defer to you simply because you are an adult—a tenuous legitimacy and one most teachers aren't comfortable with anyway. For many teachers, it is difficult to approach and correct misbehaving students they don't know, and by not correcting the behavior, the teacher implicitly condones it.

Teachers' discomfort with being asked to supervise students unknown to them in a school's common spaces is obvious in many schools. In my school in Atlanta, and in other large comprehensive schools I have visited, teachers often tacitly tolerate misbehavior in hallways that they wouldn't permit in their classrooms, such as vulgar language, inappropriate physical interactions (sexual and violent), and minor offenses such as dress code violations. Teachers in these situations simply (and often literally) look the other way or retreat to their classrooms to avoid confronting and correcting students they don't know. Avilee Goodwin, a small-school dance teacher in Oakland, California, explains: "If the students don't know me and I don't really know them, they're more likely to be hostile and resentful of me saying something to them when I was in the large school. Teachers in my large school started to not step into the hallway and say anything to students because of the big fight that would ensue, and so what they opted for was to close the door and for whatever is happening out there, let the administration handle it."

Teachers rarely have the authority or the training to feel comfortable disciplining students they do not know. Few, in fact, would want the authority or the training even if it were offered, and therefore, they cede common spaces and unstructured time to students and the school's administrators or school safety officers.

In a small school, each teacher knows a large percentage of the student population by having taught them in several

classes over multiple years and having seen them more frequently within a smaller space. When teachers are familiar
with students they aren't currently teaching, they become
more confident and comfortable holding them to expectations outside the classroom. Reciprocally, students, because they know a higher percentage of the school's adults
for the same reasons, are more likely to respond.

> LaRavian: [In the small high school] if I step into the
> hallway, everybody knows who I am, and I know who
> everybody is. The student body is small, which makes it
> really nice because you get to know not just the students
> that you teach, but you get to know the faces in the hall-
> way as they're passing by. It's like living in a small
> town—you know who people are. They know who I am,
> and I know who they are. It makes it a lot easier to step
> in the hallway and tell students to get to class or to talk
> about learning even if it's not my class. It makes a big
> difference when the person talking to you knows some-
> thing about you.

When nearly every teacher knows every student,
teachers begin to feel a collective ownership and responsibility for the entire student body, regardless of whether
they currently teach them in their classes. School expectations are enforced in all spaces and at all times, but
they are done so within a schoolwide culture of caring
and personalization built on individualized interactions
between teachers and students. Every "casual" conversation both inside and outside the classroom, between any
adult and any student, has the potential to facilitate
learning. Reprimanding a student for being noisy outside
a class in which her fellow students are taking a test is a
chance to help her see multiple perspectives and respect
the learning environment. Checking in with a student
before an upcoming test can encourage the student to
take advantage of tutoring. A concerned question posed
to a student who was absent several days the week before

can be an opportunity to discuss the difference between viral and bacterial infections and how germs are transmitted. By contrast, in a large school, investing every interaction with learning opportunities is essentially impossible when people don't know or don't feel comfortable around each other.

In all three levels of smallness—in the classroom, in the teacher's total student load, and in the school—teachers have a better opportunity to know their students and to consider this information—their individual experiences, personalities, home environments, learning styles, academic weaknesses and strengths, and interests—to improve the quality of each student's learning experiences.

This discussion presupposes that high school students, and their teachers, inherently want to build relationships with each other to facilitate effective teaching and learning. Aside from the research supporting the importance of relationships to learning, most teachers enjoy and value the relationships they build with students and the academic successes those relationships engender. And as much as they may be hesitant to admit it, high school students want and need to build relationships with trusting and reliable adults. Adolescence is an extremely stressful time, when students are wrestling with identity, ideas, values, and relationships and when the adult world looms with increased responsibility and significant pressures to be self-sufficient. Even if we teachers don't want to establish relationships with students, the students *need* us to. Moreover, when teachers know their students and are able to better meet their needs, students' greater successes give their teachers an enormous sense of accomplishment and fulfillment.

In addition to changing class size and school schedules, small schools sometimes implement additional structures to facilitate relationships between students and adults to create a schoolwide personalized environment. One such structure is the advisory, in which every adult in the school is assigned a small group of students to be their counselor, advocate, and school liaison for the students' families. In this design, parents have a specific contact at the school, and students have a resource to help them navigate the academic and social pressures of high school and plan for life beyond graduation. (For more information, see Resource C.)

Large schools don't prohibit teachers from building a relationship with a student, but having class sizes of 35 and student loads of 175, and seeing a sea of unfamiliar faces in the hallway, make it extremely difficult to do so, much less to leverage those relationships to support powerful teaching. Despite this, some teachers in large high schools are able to build relationships with more than a handful of their students. Paul Cain, a math teacher who is a former Texas Teacher of the Year, teaches in a school of over 1,800 students. On the first day of school he collects information from every student in a questionnaire, and then, beginning on the second day of school,

> I make absolutely sure that I talk with every student at least once every two days. . . . It's not just lecture in the classroom. There are lots of activities and practice problems, lots of things you can do where students either work in groups or work individually while you have an opportunity to wander around the classroom and talk to them. It doesn't have to be much; it just has to touch base with that student individually: recognizing that this young lady's a volleyball player and saying, "Hey, I saw in the paper we won," or asking a student, "Did you work late last night? You look tired this morning. What's going on?" That comment that you notice them makes a world of difference.

Paul makes it a priority to learn about his students' lives and activities outside his classroom and to use what he learns to deliberately connect with each of his students every other day. Another relationship-building strategy by teachers during the first week of school to connect and build trust with students quickly is to photograph every student on the first day of school and make flash cards to learn their names.

Alan Sitomer, a former Teacher of the Year in California who teaches at a school of 4,000 students, also recognizes the power and purpose of getting to know students and connecting with them as quickly as possible:

> My goal before the year even starts is to have high-quality relationships with all of my students: saying hello when they walk into the room and smiling at them and maybe writing a little note, or just being enthusiastic or talking about things that have nothing to do with academics but have everything to do with them as real human beings. All of those little things go such a long way, especially because they are egregiously absent in so many different areas of our own schools. You've got to recognize that in your scope of priorities as a teacher, first and foremost, you have to know your kids. That's all there is to it, and you have to remain hypersensitive to staying aware of who they are and what they're going through. Particularly being in an inner-city school, if you're not in tune to the fact that a B+ student is suddenly working at a D– level, it's easy to lose track of these kids. Having that relationship is asking, "Hey, what's going on?"

But this experience is often the exception, not the rule, in large schools. In a large school it takes a level of initiative by the student and a special personality of the teacher to build a trusting relationship. Notice that for both of these teachers in large high schools, they have an intentionality and a strategy to construct these relationships. In these cases, the relationship happens despite, not because of, the large school's structure, environment, and conditions that work to depersonalize students and teachers through large classes, large student loads, and large numbers of people in the building. Yet the more targeted and personalized the adjustment to a student's needs, the more a teacher needs to know about the student. For this reason, it is even rarer in large high schools to move beyond check-ins with every student to differentiating instruction based on knowledge about them. As we've seen, in contrast to a large school, a small school intends by its very design that teachers and students get to know and understand each other so students can be more academically successful.

POTENTIAL PITFALLS

When as a teacher you gain a deep understanding of your students—their lives, personalities, and academic needs and strengths—there are a number of possible pitfalls that most teachers have not been trained and prepared to recognize, much less to avoid.

A common mistake of teachers, especially ones new to the profession and less confident in their instruction, is that they believe they must be liked in order to be effective, and in trying to become their student's friend at the same time they are trying to be their teacher, they fail at both. In small-school environments, this situation is more likely because the school's very structure facilitates the teachers getting to know their students. Teachers in small schools can find it difficult to strike the right balance between building supportive and quasi-familial relationships with students while maintaining the appropriate distance and authority. Not only can a teacher's blurring of the distinction between teacher and friend confuse the students into thinking that there isn't any classroom hierarchy, but the teacher may find it difficult to establish authority when the need arises.

A potentially more harmful and far-reaching consequence occurs when teachers know their students so well that they compromise academic expectations. When you build relationships with students, you hear about their challenges—emotional, economic, familial, psychological, social, and physical—and can't help but feel sympathy for them when things are or have been difficult. Unfortunately, that sympathy can lead a teacher to lower her expectations and essentially exempt the struggling student from meeting academic obligations and standards. For example, if a student comes from a high-poverty family, the teacher can choose to make things "easy" on the student by demanding less of him. "It is a miracle that the student comes to school each day," the teacher might reason, "so does it really matter if he didn't get a passing score on my unit test?" The teacher falsely believes that if the student in adverse circumstances is asked to do less academically, then the pain of his circumstances will be mitigated or, perhaps, forgotten.

Compassion is certainly easier to provide, and more immediately self-satisfying for the teacher, than high-quality and empowering curriculum with sufficient supports. In extreme cases, I have seen teachers compromise professional ethics, instead adopting what I call a "culture of pity": writing students' college essays for them or grading with an overly generous curve. They feel so sorry for their students' struggles that they suspend their responsibility to prepare all students, regardless of individual circumstances, for academic mastery and self-sufficiency. Teachers in a culture of pity aren't truly serving the students' best interests, even though they believe that students are happier. Of course, some students actually might be happier when less is demanded of them. Yet although the students may seem happier, they have been given a profoundly false sense of their own readiness for life after high school. Michelle Fine calls this phenomenon "confusing hugs for calculus" (Fine 2005, 11).

Unfortunately, small-school teachers, and even an entire small-school culture, can confuse hugs for calculus. I have seen this phenomenon to be particularly evident among white, middle-class teachers who serve low-income students of color, which implicates teachers' paternalistic and ultimately racist beliefs about their students. Instead, students with struggles *need* "calculus"—a metaphor for

Sometimes teachers don't confuse hugs for calculus; they believe that students will learn calculus only if they are hugged.

the skills that can earn them opportunities to overcome their struggles—as much as, if not more than, the hugs and compassion that teachers want to provide. The teacher's beliefs and compassion can actually work against the interests of the student and the parent, because as much as the student and family may appreciate compassion, understanding, and sometimes hugs, she attends school for the calculus.

In the large school, ironically, so little is known about individual students that the academic expectations may be less likely to be compromised because of individual students' circumstances, at least based on sympathy. At the same time, however, the student in the large high school is also less likely to be known well enough to receive the support she needs to meet expectations.

Sometimes teachers don't confuse hugs for calculus; they believe that students will learn calculus only if they are hugged. In other words, teachers may mistakenly believe that relationships alone will lead to student achievement; they don't recognize that relationships are just a first step toward effective teaching and learning, not a destination.

> MICHAEL SOGUERO: Some small schools have gone to the extreme in building up good relationships, but they don't produce any results because they thought that once they got into a relationship with the students, everything would take care of itself. . . . Of course any relationship would give you a bump, but to think that that is the only thing that mattered is a false conclusion. There are a lot of technical strategies that one has to do for teaching and learning that are ignored when you only care about relationships. Schools do not produce results if they don't have a theory of teaching and learning as well and some systems to support it.

In Eagle Rock School, where Michael is principal, relationships between adults and students are a key part of the learning environment, and a means by which the school enacts its program and curriculum. Each student graduates by demonstrating success in her individualized learning plan, which is different for each student and which the teachers and students coconstruct. Courses allow for differentiated evidence of competence, and three times each year students give presentations of learning in which they present to an external panel of experts their understanding of content, skills, and personal growth in ways that reflect their own style and strengths. All of these student and teacher experiences are highly structured within the school in order to allow for minimal ambiguity around expectations but maximum flexibility on how students can meet those expectations. At this school, it is not just that students are known well in order that their needs can be met, but it is through the curriculum itself and the many choices that students have to demonstrate their understanding that students become well-known.

A final pitfall that can happen in small schools because of the emphasis on relationships is that when students trust their teachers and confide in them, teachers may treat their knowledge of students as confidential and withhold information that should be shared with the student's family. A teacher also may believe that a student's sharing of sensitive information invests the teacher with the moral authority to provide advice that may be in conflict with the family's wishes and beliefs. Teachers who know about their students may romanticize their own role as the student's "savior" and ignore the important, and legally recognized, primacy of parents and guardians in a student's upbringing. Similarly, the teacher who has built a relationship with students may have an unrealistic appreciation of her own limitations; students may share information and have needs that are best addressed by a therapist or social worker with specialized training and expertise. It can be difficult for a teacher who is intimately aware of a student's life and needs, and who feels responsible for helping the student, to be modest enough about her own lack of expertise to refer students to the assistance of other adults who don't know the student as well.

While I have seen many small schools experience these pitfalls, often not only in individual classrooms but throughout their entire culture, I have rarely seen them in large schools because their organizational systems and structures are not designed to support relationships. When these dynamics do happen in large schools, it is by individual teachers who, despite their work context, try to construct relationships with and a deep understanding of their students—what small schools try to do.

CONCLUSION

When I had almost 3,000 students in my high school, of course I wanted to know every single student as a learner. It was tough after four years to even know them by first and last name, let alone who they were as people and what they needed as learners. Yet at my small school where I have less than 400 students, I know every single student, I know their family, I know who they are as learners, I know what their goals and dreams and aspirations are in regards to college and post-secondary learning. I know who struggles with reading, who loves math. I know who is a scientific thinker. You know because you have stronger, more personalized relationships with them as people and as learners. And that provides a richer context for both adults and students in the building. (Stacy Spector, former small-school teacher and principal, Citrus Heights, California)

In small-school classrooms, teachers can learn about their students more deeply than is possible in a large school. Teachers can tailor their interactions and approaches to instruction when they know the contexts that students bring to their learning experiences. They can select specific content, materials, activities, and assessments that meet each student's needs and respond to the student's interests. Students recognize and value these relationships and are more likely to respond to the teachers who know them and to be invested in a school that treats them as individuals. With these personalized connections with students, teachers become more invested in their students' success, and with a clear understanding of each student's needs, strengths, and interests, they can do something about it. Nevertheless, teachers need to be attuned to their psychological reactions to this deeper knowledge of students so that they don't compromise expectations or their own professional commitments.

A theme throughout this book is that small schools create the conditions for powerful experiences for students and teachers, but the size of a school by itself does not guarantee those benefits. As Nancy Mohr writes, "It might be argued that if a school is small, even if nothing else changes, it will allow its teachers and students to know each other better. And that would be true. But toward what end?" (2000, 142). While it can be relatively easy for teachers to take advantage of the size of a small school to connect with students interpersonally, it is much more difficult to take full and consistent advantage of the powerful teaching and learning opportunities that small schools allow. Yet this is really the only purpose for knowing students: to improve their opportunities to be academically successful. Teachers in some schools may settle for a *personalized environment* but not push themselves and their students to create *personalized learning*; in other words, they may settle for hugs and ignore calculus. They may ignore the possibilities for teaching and learning and choose instead to create teacher-centered lessons, to use a narrow range of assessments, and to implement a one-size-fits-all curriculum, all common in large schools because of their bureaucratic orientation. They may choose to distance themselves from students and see them simply as a collection of teenagers on whose shoulders rest the obligation to learn. Those teachers' classrooms, even though they may be in small schools, will seem no different from those in larger schools, and student experiences will also be no different.

In this chapter we focused on how having fewer students can change an individual teacher's relationship to the students he or she interacts with. To leverage the teacher-student relationships possible in a small school in order to improve learning requires a paradigm shift in what happens in a classroom—how curriculum is developed, what instruction looks like, and how students participate in their learning—and a teacher can't do it alone in a single classroom. Fortunately, though smallness greatly influences the quality of relationships between teachers and their students, the real power of a small school to improve student achievement is through how it facilitates relationships among its teachers.

In the next chapter, we open the classroom door and explore how teachers in small schools work with each other to support teaching and learning opportunities.

DISCUSSION QUESTIONS

1. Consider your own past, current, and future work with students. How has, does, or will knowing students change your work with them?

2. This chapter discusses the benefits of teachers building relationships to know their students. What are the benefits of teachers making themselves knowable to students? What are the benefits of students knowing each other?

3. Based on what you know about how school size affects relationships between teachers and students, what predictions can you make about how having fewer adults in a school can affect their relationships and change their work?

4. How might a teacher negotiate the blurry boundary between knowing too little and knowing too much about a student? What might it look like and involve to know a student "well enough" to make one's teaching authentic, caring, and responsive to that student's needs?

FURTHER READING

Advisory Resources on the Coalition of Essential Schools. 2009. http://www.essentialschools.org.

Delpit, Lisa. 1995. *Other People's Children: Cultural Conflict in the Classroom.* New York: New Press.

Eagle Rock School. 2009. http://www.eaglerockschool.org/home/index.asp.

Fine, Michelle. 2005. "Not in Our Name: Reclaiming the Democratic Vision of Small School Reform." *Rethinking Schools* 19, 4: 11–14.

Gay, Geneva. 2000. *Culturally Responsive Teaching: Theory, Research, and Practice.* Multicultural Education Series. New York: Teachers College Press.

Tomlinson, Carol Ann, and Cindy A. Strickland. 2005. *Differentiation in Practice: A Resource Guide for Differentiating Curriculum, Grades 9–12.* Alexandria, VA: Association for Supervision and Curriculum Development.

CHAPTER THREE

THE TEACHER'S EXPERIENCE IN A SMALL SCHOOL

Relationships with Other Teachers

ROM MY JOURNAL during my first year of teaching:

It's great to be able to walk next door to Randy's room or across the hall to David's room to talk about what's happening in our classrooms or just to chew the fat. Randy and I, because we both teach U.S. History, talk about our curriculum, and although we take very different approaches to the subject, we shared some primary source texts today about the Trail of Tears. Because David and I both teach 9th graders (he teaches science), we talk about students we have in common. Today we spoke about Travon, a student we both struggle with every day. We seem to have some similar problems with him—he cracks jokes and gets other students off task, and he gets angry very quickly when he gets frustrated—and we talked about different strategies we have tried, mostly unsuccessfully.

What I really appreciate about these interactions is not just being able to talk with an adult during the day, which sometimes is so important. We're able to help each other and therefore affect those students who aren't even in our own classes.

But sometimes it seems like we're just scratching the surface: We only really talk during passing periods because we don't share the same prep period or talk much during lunch (we all have our own students who come in our classrooms at lunchtime), so we don't have much opportunity to really get deep into any discussion. Randy and I, although we both teach the same subject, don't really know what each other is doing, and neither David nor I really know what Travon is doing in the other's class, or how each of us is reacting, so all we do is share experiences and brainstorm. I guess at least it helps us each not to feel so alone in our work. And when it seems like I'm spending 12 hours a day at or with work, to connect with colleagues, in any way, feels important.

In this excerpt, I valued talking with two of my fellow teachers—both of whom were, like me, relatively new to teaching—but what was I looking for? With Randy, I wanted to improve how I taught U.S. history, and that meant finding additional classroom materials. But although collecting curriculum is certainly critical for a new teacher, we didn't have a way to enhance each other's instruction. David and I vented about our experiences with one student, but we were only two out of seven teachers who saw Travon each day. In neither case did we really know what was happening in each other's classrooms, and without guidance on how to talk about our teaching, and formalized time to do so, how much could we learn from each other? What could the school have done to help us to have these conversations, and how much did the size of our school matter?

The last chapter focused on the value of teacher-student relationships for student learning and how school structures can foster and facilitate, or impede and prohibit, these relationships. A school with fewer students provides more opportunities for students and their teachers to know each other and therefore more powerful ways for teachers to support student success. And just as small high schools create conditions for teachers to build relationships with students—with small class sizes, smaller class loads, and smaller total student bodies—they can also create ways for teachers to build relationships with each other, enabling them to grow from and with each other and, in the end, to serve their students more effectively. This chapter will explore those opportunities.

THE TRADITIONAL CONTEXT OF TEACHERS' WORK

Most teachers in secondary schools, since the advent of the comprehensive factory model of high schools, have worked in isolated conditions. Dan Lortie, in his seminal work, *Schoolteacher* (1975), likened the interior design of schools to an egg carton. Each classroom is separated from others while joined together, one after the other, only for convenience and economy, an architectural design that effectively structures fragmented individualism into the teaching profession. Teachers work in isolation not only because of the school's physical design but also because of the historical understanding of the teaching profession. Tony Wagner writes, "As in the well-designed, efficient factory of the early 20th century, each [teacher] is believed to provide the optimal contribution to the whole when she focuses entirely on her own responsibilities" (2001, 379). Teachers are specialized technical workers, each responsible for teaching a particular set of skills and content, and students are the manufactured "product" on the assembly line as they progress from one teacher's class to the next.

Isolation is not just imposed on teachers by the physical layout of schools or the conception of the teacher as assembly-line worker. Teachers can desire isolation in order to fend off bureaucratic demands and restrictions in traditional school environments. Externally imposed "teacher-proof" curriculum, regulatory requirements, and mercurial administrative mandates, combined with the varied goals of the job, growing pressures for accountability, and teachers' commitment to their work, lead teachers to construct and cherish isolation. Many teachers close their classroom doors to protect themselves from demands they view as disconnected from and constraining their work and their students' needs.

This isolation emerges in part from a history of teacher autonomy. Judith Warren Little asserts that this autonomy rests on "freedom from scrutiny and the largely unexamined right to exercise personal preference" (1990, 513). Wagner writes that teaching has been a "craftsman's" trade and has attracted people who enjoy working alone and being left alone and who take great pride in developing a degree of expertise and in perfecting "handcrafted products" (2001, 379). With the shield of "academic freedom," many teachers protect their curriculum, along with the time, energy, and ownership invested in that curriculum, although sometimes this is done to protect curriculum for its meaning and value to the teacher, independent of its meaning and value for students.

But teachers' isolation doesn't insulate them only from the bureaucracy; because most teachers work independently, their work becomes hidden from their peers and even unreviewable by them. Little continues her description of teacher isolation by explaining that "teachers acknowledge and tolerate the individual preferences or styles of others" (1990, 513). Within the traditional school's pervasive culture of isolation and individual autonomy, teachers rarely initiate discussions about teaching and learning with each other. Little argues that because autonomy is so highly valued among teachers, teachers become reluctant to engage in conversations that could suggest an intrusion into another teacher's practice. Unless one teacher specifically asks for assistance, engaging in discussions that expose one's practice and involve feedback suggests a challenge to teacher competence:

> Teachers carefully preserve the boundary between offering advice when asked and interfering in unwarranted ways in another teacher's work. Most teachers expect to supply advice when asked—and only when asked. . . . Discussion about practices of teaching, under such circumstances, becomes difficult to separate from judgments of the competence of teachers. Understandably, teachers may show little inclination to engage with peers around matters of curriculum and instruction if doing so can only be managed in ways that may jeopardize self-esteem and professional standing. (Little 1990, 515–516)

The shield teachers use against outside interference therefore can become a sword against peer contribution and collective growth and can create a schoolwide culture in which teachers don't talk about their own work or hear about others'. The external (and often self-imposed) pressures to be effective, combined with the daily frustrations of meeting student needs, with no opportunities to receive meaningful feedback to improve, can threaten teachers' confidence and security. Consequently, when others engage them in conversations about their practice, teachers may "defend their collective sense of competence in the face of potentially discrediting evidence . . . posed by the behavior of pupils" (Hammersly 1984, 212).

I don't mean to suggest a purely deficit model of teachers' traditional work experiences. Hargreaves suggests that isolation helps many teachers not only fend off intrusive bureaucracies but also maintain a sense of self in the depersonalizing environment of traditional schools

(Hargreaves 1994, 30). And as we will see, particularly inspired and motivated teachers, regardless of the school size in which they work, can find peer support through relationships they initiate within the school or outside of it. The question is, how do large and small high schools support teacher interactions that improve practice within the entrenched culture of teacher isolation?

RELATIONSHIPS AMONG TEACHERS IN LARGE HIGH SCHOOLS

Large high schools have traditional designs and structures that generally impede meaningful interactions among teachers. In large-high-school facilities, teachers are spread out across multiple hallways and floors, usually with no strategic assignment other than to ensure that science and art teachers are in classrooms with sinks. With limited nonteaching time during the day, teachers interact most conveniently with colleagues in nearby classrooms, who may or may not teach any common content or common students. At times, teachers will make the effort to seek out colleagues across the expanse of the campus or building, but because secondary teachers have specialized content, and in large schools rarely share students, they have little in common to talk about. Therefore, informal interactions with colleagues—what R. J. Campbell calls "snatched time" (Hargreaves 1994, 97)—in the hallway, staff lounge, copy room, or parking lot are about topics other than students and classrooms. I spoke with two teachers who had taught in large schools whose experiences reflect this:

> STACIE PIERPOINT: At the large school I was at, I never saw teachers that were in other parts of the building just because of the way the physical space was laid out. Even within my Spanish department, people didn't really talk. They just crossed paths, and then at lunchtime everybody would meet in the teachers' room and just gripe.

AVILEE: At my old school [that was large] we would have groups of teachers that sat together at lunch, and we would talk about anything except what's going on with the kids. They'd talk about what was on television last night.

Both Stacie and Avilee struggled to interact with colleagues in ways that they believed could improve their practice. One explanation for their experiences is that in large schools, the more faculty members, the harder it is to find common needs, interests, and classroom contexts for teachers to talk about with each other. When each teacher knows only her own classroom, perspectives are narrow and independent. Unless teachers recognize common interests, struggles, and needs, what else would we expect them to talk about besides television last night? If we know that teachers' work needs to be "deprivatized"—in which teachers talk with each other about their classrooms and the teaching and learning that happen there—why do many large high schools find it so difficult to do so?

The first hindrance to developing a collaborative culture in large high schools is that such a culture depends on relationships among the adults. Large schools have large numbers of teachers, and it becomes hard for them to know each other well, or to be known as individuals. The work environment can become as impersonal for teachers as it is for students. In large high schools, it is not unusual for teachers who have worked there for decades to know only a handful of the faculty by name. LaRavian Battle recalls her work in a comprehensive school: "The school was so large that no one really knew anybody. Everybody didn't know each other on a personal level. Even the teachers had cliques." When teachers don't have relationships with each other, and therefore don't trust each other, it's hard for them to feel comfortable sharing classroom experiences and speaking meaningfully about teaching and learning.

In faculty meetings in many large high schools, when teachers have dedicated time to be with each other, the only commonality among them, or at least the only one exposed, is that they all work in the same building. To build commonality among so many teachers takes time and deft facilitation (if it is even possible), and many administrators opt to use faculty meetings to ensure that all staff follow the school's bureaucratic procedures and systems. The bureaucracy everyone works in becomes what everyone has in common, and it becomes no coincidence that this bureaucracy and the frustrations with it become the focus, and even the purpose, of teacher interactions in large comprehensive schools.

Many large schools do little to facilitate meaningful relationship-building beyond the informal happy hour or holiday party. Teachers are not encouraged or trained to visit other classrooms. Because administrators in large schools are often consumed with making sure the bureaucracy runs efficiently, and because their schools have so many faculty, their infrequent visits to teachers' classrooms are usually only for evaluative purposes. As a result of these two dynamics, visits by any adults in teachers' classrooms have the suggestion of evaluation, inhibiting teachers' willingness to observe peers.

Given the deeply rooted context of teachers' work and the ways large high schools reinforce traditional dispositions and behaviors about their work, how are small schools poised to reorganize and restructure teachers' experiences with colleagues, and how do those relationships affect the classroom?

TEACHERS' STRUCTURED RELATIONSHIPS IN SMALL SCHOOLS

Just as we learned that relationships between students and teachers are important to student learning, when teachers have peer relationships, they are more likely to learn from and with each other, to trust each other, and to support each other. Relationships enable teachers to know students as individuals, to care for them and recognize strengths and weaknesses; relationships among teachers work the same way. When teachers know each other not only as individual and "whole" people but also as fellow teaching professionals, they can identify and draw upon each other's expertise, build on each other's ideas, and work together to improve teaching and learning throughout the school. For example, in a school where teachers know and have relationships with each other, a teacher who struggles with a particular lesson or classroom management strategy will be more likely to know which of her peers to turn to for assistance and, perhaps more importantly, will feel more comfortable admitting to that teacher that she is struggling. Other teachers who know that teacher well—her background, her strengths, her weaknesses—will be able to provide more thoughtful and individualized support that addresses her needs as well as her learning style.

In small high schools, because of the small number of teachers and the smaller size of the school, relationships can develop informally:

STACIE PIERPOINT: It amazed me—at the one school I was at [a large comprehensive school]—we had our meetings in a huge auditorium, and there were just so many people in there that people just gave you information and then you left. Because [my current school is] smaller, teachers see each other more often on a daily basis, so there's already more of a chance that teachers will have relationships with each other. Teachers tend to know each other more and feel more comfortable with each other instead of being a stranger in the same building. There's less isolation in the classroom—like you go to your classroom, do what you need to do, and then leave—because you're more likely to run into another teacher and have a discussion.

Simply working in a smaller physical space can facilitate interactions and familiarity among colleagues; there just aren't that many places to go.

Though small schools, by being small, can create familiarity among teachers because a teacher is more "likely to run into another teacher," having a small number of teachers creates opportunities to build relationships through structures that facilitate meaningful work among colleagues. Just as fewer students in a classroom means that students can get to know each other through learning activities, fewer faculty in a school means that they can build relationships through thoughtfully planned interactions. It is those structured and intentional interactions among teachers, much more possible in small schools with fewer faculty, that promote what Little calls "joint work" (1990, 519). Juxtaposed against the traditional model of teachers' work environments—in which teachers are isolated, are independently autonomous, and have experiences and interests that are limited to their own classroom—joint work consists of "encounters among teachers that rest on shared responsibility for the work of teaching (interdependence), collective conceptions of autonomy, support for teachers' initiative and leadership with regard to professional practice, and group affiliations grounded in professional work" (Little 1990, 519).

One key way that small schools facilitate the intentional interactions that engage in Little's joint work is by engendering shared interests among teachers. Large schools, with so many teachers, programs, tracks, and interests, make it difficult to incentivize teachers to work collaboratively even if they do know each other; each one has very disparate interests. Small schools promote teacher collaboration in part because teachers in small schools have many shared interests and therefore are motivated to work together to further those common interests. So how do small schools tap into and generate shared interests among teachers, and then utilize those interests to facilitate meaningful conversations and joint work?

First, teachers in small schools are likely to *share a common student*. When a teacher struggles with a specific student and wants help from a colleague, it is difficult for the advice to be meaningful if the colleague hasn't taught that student. The helpful colleague can only group the student into a category of students based on the struggling teacher's description and the colleague's previous students: "unmotivated," "defiant," "truant," "poor reader," "easily distracted." The colleague's advice will be generic ("put her in the front of the room") and most likely unsatisfying for the struggling teacher. In a large school, say of 2,500 students, where students have six or seven teachers a day among a faculty of a hundred, it is difficult for the struggling teacher to find one of the other teachers who teach that student who is also both available and someone from whom the struggling teacher feels comfortable asking for advice.

In a small school, if students have six teachers a day, but there are only twenty-five teachers, there's a much higher likelihood that colleagues will know the student discussed. Their advice about how to address the student's needs will be more relevant and valuable to the struggling teacher; other teachers may have had successes with particular classroom management strategies or may know the student's skill deficits, interests, or learning style. Avilee talks about how smallness enables teachers to easily identify which of their colleagues have shared interests:

> You can walk into the staff room and ask, "How's M—
> doing today?" and everyone knows who has which stu-
> dents because it's a pretty small staff. We know that if
> I've got juniors they must have Ms. C— because they all
> have American history. I immediately know which social
> science teacher they have because there's only one that
> teaches American history so I can walk over to Ms.
> C—'s class and say, "Was there something strange about
> M—today? Because she was acting like this in my class."

I have found that it becomes much more likely in small schools that teachers will share advice to address student-specific challenges not only because it is easier to identify which teachers teach or have taught each student but because teachers have relationships with their colleagues that make them comfortable with asking for assistance.

In small schools, because there are fewer teachers, more teachers share more students, which can create a shared need among them for purposeful conversations. Heather Cristol, a small-school English teacher in Brooklyn, New York, says,

> All the advisors of the twelfth grade meet regularly, as a grade team and as an English department. I don't think you can do that in a large school, where you have so many more students and so many sections of everything. So we can communicate about students from year to year and during the year about how they're doing in all of their subjects and coordinate our effort to help them in a way that I don't think you can do when you have the sheer numbers that you tend to have at a [large] school.

(See Resource C for more information on advisories in small schools.)

Beyond simply sharing advice, teachers who share the same student can coordinate their efforts to work at common purposes so that students succeed. Instead of each teacher working individually using unique strategies, teachers can pool their information and experiences with that student to organize a common approach to address that student's needs. For example, teachers can create a behavior management strategy for the student that applies consistently across all of that student's classes, or they can identify information about the student that affects the student's learning in order to collectively accommodate the student's circumstances. In one school I visited, there was a student who stayed at a different relative's house nearly each day and who, when she left homework at one house, would not be able to get it until the next week. The teachers of that student agreed to have the student stay after school to complete homework and to provide a space in each classroom for the student to leave her class materials rather than take them home.

Fenway School in Boston is one small school that clusters teachers and students, and adults meet periodically to plan how to collaboratively support individual struggling students, a practice that Ann Lieberman describes as a "descriptive review process" (1995, 594). As teachers work together and invest time and energy in helping the student, they begin not only to develop a sense of shared responsibility for the student's achievement but also to depend and rely on each other, building mutual trust and shared confidence.

Large schools, with their wide array of academic tracks, special programs, and electives, generally find it impracticable to gather teachers to discuss shared students, except when the student is experiencing a crisis or when the law demands it, such as for IEP (Individualized Education Program) meetings, in which the student's teachers develop and implement a unified plan for the student's success. Sharing information about common students otherwise seldom occurs in large schools simply because of the logistical difficulties of getting teachers with so many disparate schedules together at one time.

Beyond sharing a single common student among teachers, small schools can deliberately structure their schedules so that a team of teachers shares a group of students, which creates even more powerful opportunities for teacher collaboration. In addition to being able to share information and to create common strategies for individual cases, teachers can work with each other to harmonize their vision for teaching and learning and create a coherence among their classes that enhances the collective educational experience of students in each classroom.

To really understand the impact of instructional coherence on teachers who share students, let's view a school day from a student's perspective. In most large high schools, as a student moves through a series of classes each day, he is asked to work with multiple teachers, each with her own style and expectations. Each classroom has its own procedures, rules for behavior, content and skill emphases, and instructional strategies. The student is expected to remember and successfully switch mental gears from class to class and correctly sort the dozens and even hundreds of explicit and implicit expectations comprising each classroom's context. Because a teacher's grades usually reflect not only a student's content mastery but also how well he meets expectations in that context, a student's academic success in school is often largely dependent on his facility for remembering and adhering to several sets of distinct and sometimes contradictory rules, procedures, and expectations. He must remember which teacher requires paper headings on the right side, which teacher prefers staples over paper clips, which teacher requires that students raise their hands before they can answer, and in which class the students can't get up from their seats until the teacher dismisses them. Besides the procedures of classrooms, a student has to remember each teacher's policies: how many tardies are allowed, when late homework is accepted, how much class participation matters, and how (and if) tests can be retaken. Then, even if the student can keep straight all of the procedures and policies, he must successfully meet each teacher's academic expectations: what makes for an appropriate sentence, paragraph, or essay, and whether students are rewarded for synthesizing ideas and questioning assumptions or for memorizing facts and recalling lectures.

When viewed from the student's perspective, this kind of school day seems fragmented, an environment in which we would never ask adults to function: to work with several supervisors, each requiring different behaviors and expecting varying levels of performance, with those requirements switching every hour, and with each supervisor ignorant of the others' expectations. Unfortunately, this is the learning environment that most traditional high schools construct, which clearly creates additional, and unnecessary, hurdles for students.

This structure increases the burden not only on the student. When teachers each have distinct rules and expectations, they create more work for each other; each must spend significant time developing, explaining, reminding, and enforcing her own rules and expectations, which often contradict every other teacher's. It takes students much longer to learn my expectations, and it takes me much longer to teach them, because I'm competing against every other teacher's differing expectations.

In small schools, because the small number of students makes it easy to assign a group of students to a group of teachers, teachers can, in addition to sharing information and strategies to help individual students, share common expectations for students. Stacie Pierpoint explains: "[In a small school] everyone has similar expectations of what the students should be doing in the classroom, what learning should look like in the classroom, what student behavior should look like in the classroom. If teachers are all over the place with their behavior management, students will spend time trying to see what they can get away with in each classroom."

When teachers can agree on procedures and expectations, students need only learn one set of rules, and with every teacher enforcing the same rules, the students learn them quickly. If every one of a student's teachers has the same policy for accepting late work, that is the only expectation about late work that needs to be learned, and the student can be held accountable for it within days instead of months. Each teacher supports, rather than undermines, the expectations of the others, which allows them to focus their energies on the content and skills of the class, not the rules for its operation.

In addition to common agreements about class policies, teachers share academic expectations through the identification of connections and overlap between their content areas.

> AVILEE: This year in the dance production class our focus is working with dance as a way to work with text and words, and for the dance festival we were able to collaborate with our freshman English teacher, who is a spoken word artist and performance poet. If I didn't know him pretty well, we wouldn't have been able to do that because I wouldn't have any idea that Mr. C— is such a wonderful performance poet. I never would have even thought of it.

Building on her relationships and familiarity with her peers, Avilee made connections between her subject area and another teacher's to build cross-curriculum experiences for her students. Students learned about dance and words as interactive and complementary expressions of ideas. This sharing of academic expectations for the dance festival came about informally, through two teachers getting to know each other, but it can also happen more deliberately. Teachers who share students can agree on the important skills and how they will be taught across the entire grade level so students strengthen those skills across all subject areas.

For example, English teachers are usually expected to have sole responsibility to teach writing skills, arguably one of the most important skills that students learn in school. When teachers share expectations for writing skills, rather than delegating them to the English teacher, the responsibility for teaching those skills becomes shared among all of the teachers. Each teacher emphasizes writing and supports common expectations for writing competency, and those skills are woven through all parts of the students' day.

LaRavian talks about her small school's team approach to writing instruction:

One of the problems in high school—one of the gaps—
is that students are graduating not knowing how to write
very well. So we're trying to figure out why that is and
why we're dropping the ball. And getting at that is
breaking down what should they know in the ninth
grade, what should they know in the tenth grade, and so
forth. And then, if we can figure out what exactly it is
that students should be able to do by the time they leave
the ninth grade, then we can divide up those writing assignments across the curriculum. Everybody's vested in
getting our students to write better, so you can break
down what each teacher should be doing to address the
lack of writing skills. Being able to talk about those
ideas—what a good paper looks like and the different
styles—is very important.

While her thinking is impressive in its own right, what
makes it particularly powerful is that she is an algebra
teacher. When teachers who share students agree on academic expectations, they can focus themselves and their
students on the most critical cross-curriculum skills, and
just as shared behavioral expectations ease the individual
work of each teacher to teach rules, shared academic expectations and instructional strategies create distributed
and collectively reinforced support of key academic skills
among all of the teachers. This shared responsibility for
common students rarely happens in large high schools,
where instead each teacher views her role as to serve only
her own students within her own specific subject, and
she must do so alone. In small schools, because teachers
know each other and have built relationships with students, and especially when they are organized to teach a
common set of students, they feel a shared responsibility
to collectively serve their students.

In small schools where teachers establish relationships
and recognize their shared responsibility, and when they
create structures to support teacher growth through

common prep periods or planning time, teachers feel safe enough to deprivatize their classroom practices. Teachers value a reflective review of their work alongside their colleagues, subjugating their own individual personal and professional insecurities to the needs of their students, the goals of their professional community, and the learning culture of the school. Stacy Spector describes the contrasting atmospheres among teachers:

> It's a place of safety . . . to support one another as learners, and not a place where I have to have the right lesson, the perfect students, and a teacher or an administrator is going to come in with a checklist of "I gotcha's." Instead it's teachers sitting around a table saying, "How do we know our students as learners? In what ways do they learn best? How do we set up the conditions for that to happen? How do we model those?" In a small school when you have people who know each other as adult learners, it allows you to be more attentive to that and it makes your practice better and smarter.

Stacy and her colleagues have moved beyond the traditional disposition of teachers, in which, according to Hargreaves, they are so isolated and depersonalized that there is a secrecy of practice. When teachers are expected to grow and become better teachers primarily on their own, in their own isolated context, "independent trial and error serves as the principal route to competence" (1994, 513).

Little describes, in contrast to the isolation and insulation from critique teachers normally experience, how joint work, rather than creating a culture of insecurity, validates teachers' expertise and skills in authentic ways: "Teachers open their intentions and practices to public examination, but in turn are credited for their knowledge, skill, and judgment. Indeed, the close scrutiny of practice within a group perhaps is sustained where the competence and commitment of the members are not in doubt" (1990, 521). This level of transparency and trust among colleagues that Stacy describes requires and strengthens teachers' confidence in their own capacities to learn and grow as a community. Their interdependence means that they must provide support and accept support so that all teachers have effective teaching and learning with common expectations for students and themselves. And this can happen in small schools most easily because of both the collegial relationships that can develop and the opportunity to generate shared interests.

But this mind-set is a radical shift for teachers, whose work has always been private, and the difficulty of getting teachers to have meaningful conversations about what they do in classrooms cannot be understated. Mary Beth Blegen, 1996 National Teacher of the Year, who has visited and worked with hundreds of schools, explains:

> The "how to" piece of having conversations is much harder than we would have imagined. Having authentic conversations about student learning, curriculum, teaching, and assessments means retooling the mind-set of teachers who are used to being independent contractors. This means that teachers have to desist from taking conversations personally, that they begin to look at everything from the standpoint of learning rather than teaching, and that they practice true collaborative skills . . . none of which come naturally or easily.

Small schools may make it inevitable that adults will get to know each other, but simply knowing colleagues doesn't necessarily make Little's concept of joint work emerge "naturally or easily." Just as teachers in small schools can mistakenly believe that personalized teacher-student relationships alone lead to student achievement, some small-school teachers believe that their "smallness," in which teachers know each other and enjoy comfortable relationships with each other, translates automatically into a professional learning community. Being comfortable with peers doesn't mean that teachers have a reason or have the skills to work with each other around shared purposes; professional isolation can still be the prevailing culture even when teachers have personal connections with each other. Peter Ross describes what is required for schools to move beyond relationships to the authentic conversations that improve teacher practice and student learning:

> You can have a small school where there is a very lax professional culture and people just want to be buddies with each other and buddies with the kids and everybody wants to personalize everything . . . but you might not be getting the rigorous results that you could get if you married all of that personalization with a strong rigorous professional culture and some high standards and some accountability for each other. You need to go through the hard work of norming what a quality piece of work looks like; you need to have it formalized that you actually collaborate, that you actually visit people's classroom, that you actually critique people's teaching and instruction. Once you start going down that path of "we've got some formal structures, we've got some norms, we all agree we're here to learn from each other, that we're going to give each other constructive criticism," then you can start ratcheting up what you expect of each other and ultimately what you expect of the kids, and that's when you can start to get traction.

For LaRavian, this has created a powerful dynamic of mutual support:

> In my small school, everybody's on the same page with students' grades and scores and how they're achieving. Everybody's looking at data, and everybody's sharing ideas on how to make all of our students achieve better than they were before. And I think the feeling of community within my school, and that positive peer pressure from my colleagues, have helped make me a better

teacher and much more vested in my students. There is the sense of community we have created in our small school that was lacking in the large school because nobody really knew anybody.

Recognizing shared interests (we collectively share a group of students) creates the need for mutual support (it's important that we help each other become better teachers), and because we are all working together toward a common goal with common students, we are dependent on each other (everybody's sharing ideas) and mutually accountable to each other (we exert positive peer pressure).

For this reason, the most successful small schools are intentional about creating a culture of joint work. They establish formalized rules and behaviors for their interactions: clear processes for teachers watching each other teach, protocols for conversations, and standard ways of identifying student performance as evidence of teachers' work. Rules and protocols establish safe spaces for teachers to have these difficult and authentic conversations, and shift the orientation among the adults from the teacher's experience—what am I doing in my classroom?—to the students' experiences—what learning are they demonstrating?

The Coalition of Essential Schools, for example, has done significant work on developing such protocols for teachers. In large schools, data analysis is often limited to schoolwide averages or trends among large groups of students. When there are fewer students, and teachers have established a culture of using student evidence to inform practice, data become much more granular, focusing on student work on a single assignment or students' demonstration of meeting some agreed-on benchmark. (For an example of a protocol for looking at student work, see Resource D.) Small-school teachers, because they know their students so well, are also positioned to analyze student growth rather than just outcomes—asking not only,

TEXTBOX 3.1 COALITION OF ESSENTIAL SCHOOLS

CES was established in 1984 based on the school reform principles described in Theodore Sizer's pivotal work, *Horace's Compromise: The Dilemma of the American High School* (1984). It has membership schools throughout the country that subscribe to ten "Common Principles" drawn from Sizer's book (CES 2006):

- Learning to use one's mind well
- Less is more, depth over coverage
- Goals apply to all students
- Personalization
- Student-as-worker, teacher-as-coach
- Demonstration of mastery
- A tone of decency and trust
- Commitment to the entire school
- Resources dedicated to teaching and learning
- Democracy and equity (this principle was added later, in the mid-nineties)

For more information, see http://www.essentialschools.org.

"How many of my students attained competency in the targeted skill?" but also "What was the increase in each individual student's competency, and how do student experiences in my class compare with students' experiences in my colleagues' classrooms?" In other words, the faculty constructs and implements a plan for professional learning with clear norms and expectations that has the same level of rigor, detail, and accountability that teachers strive to create for students.

Focus point   Peter Ross frames the progression of professional community as such: *"Smallness creates intimacy, the intimacy creates transparency, and the transparency hopefully creates mutual accountability."* When teachers depend on their collective practices to be as effective as possible, they agree to be accountable to each other and to assess the quality of practice according to common student outcomes. As Stacy Spector describes a small school:

> There's an accountability that I can't just talk a good game, I have to be able to demonstrate evidence of student learning as a result of decisions that I have made in my classroom. . . . I think that changes the game from a comprehensive high school model, where "Oh yeah, my kids are getting it," and maybe you look at standardized data maybe once a year as a means to inform your practice, whereas in a small school you're looking at a variety of data, and not just standardized ones, to inform your practice. . . . That changes the dynamic of learning in the building.

Of course, no stage of this evolution—from strategizing together about helping shared individual students, to considering common expectations for shared groups of students, to recognizing interdependencies among teachers for those students' success, to deprivatizing classroom practice, and finally to institutionalizing a constructive, critical, and supportive learning community of teachers— is automatic in small schools. Yet each element is more likely to occur in a small school where a small number of adults know each other and their students.

An added consequence when small schools establish this learning environment for adults is that it models the approach to learning that small schools can create for students. When sharing and joint work are woven into the school's professional culture, teachers' practices of collaborative adult learning help them create classrooms of collaborative learning as well, both during and outside class time:

STACIE PIERPOINT: A lot of times after school, kids were getting help in different classrooms, and it was very

obvious that teachers were working together. Teachers
would go into those classrooms and talk to other teachers, asking questions such as: "I'm doing this lesson
plan. What do you think would be the best way to do
this?" It's helpful for students to see adults asking questions, taking risks, and working together as models for
how to interact with each other and how to be part of a
team and help each other out . . . just knowing that at
every stage of life, whether you're an adult or a child,
you're still a learner.

Stacie reminds us that the students are always watching
us, and it is worth considering how teachers who experience isolation or collaboration in their own work are
likely to teach their students to work in similar ways, either through instruction or through modeling. If teachers work entirely in isolation, how can they be expected
to teach students how to collaborate with each other and
the value of doing so?

In most schools, the school's education program is a
mix of expectations that reflect the individual philoso-
phy, vision, content knowledge, and teaching skill of
each teacher. Through knowing each other, making their
work transparent, sharing accountability for their shared
students, and being intentional about how they support
each other to increase student achievement, teachers can
feel collectively responsible for effecting their common
goals.

CONSTRUCTING TEACHER
COLLABORATION IN LARGE SCHOOLS

Because they cannot organize their students and teachers
as small schools do, large schools find other ways to organize their faculty, usually by subject-area departments.
When the teachers in the department share content, not
students, and the school does not facilitate relationships,
a culture of transparency, safety, or shared purposes or interests for teaching and learning, meetings too often ad-

dress only the group's common administrative interests, such as ordering sufficient textbooks or scheduling exams, and students are discussed abstractly, if at all.

Nevertheless, it is possible in large schools to create a professional culture of collaboration, most likely within a subject department. Paul Cain, a former Texas Teacher of the Year, was head of his large school's math department for many years and established a professional culture among the math teachers. The fifteen math teachers have lunch together, celebrate monthly birthday dinners, and frequently recognize each other's achievements. He also structured teaching assignments to create the need for teachers to work collaboratively: of his fifteen teachers, thirteen teach Algebra I to ninth graders and struggling students in higher grades, a strategy that created, he says, "a very large pool of teachers helping our least motivated students."

Having encouraged camaraderie among the department's teachers and then implemented course assignments that created shared interests, he constructed a culture of mutual support in which teachers aren't afraid to ask for help and to learn from each other:

> In our department, teachers walk into my room in the middle of class and sit down in the back of the classroom, and nobody even thinks about it. I can walk into another teacher's classroom, sit down, visit with her students, and the whole idea is that it's safe. It's comfortable—it's not stepping on somebody else's territory. We're always sharing information. Very often, half the department's eating lunch in the math lab, and you look over someone's shoulder, and they're doing a worksheet, and you say, "Hey, that's pretty cool; can I see a copy of that?" and somebody will print it out. We're swapping information constantly in an informal manner, which means you don't have to say, "Gee, I'm dumb; can you help me with this?" It's just a matter of courtesy that you're working with a bunch of professionals, and we share virtually everything.

Through the unusual move of having nearly all teachers in the department teach the same course, Paul fostered a collegial environment with norms (although informal) that challenge teachers' traditional isolation. He generated shared interests among the majority of the department to talk about how to effectively teach algebra.

In contrast to the large school's focus on subject departments as its primary context for teacher conversations, I have seen small schools that completely ignore the shared interests among content-area teachers—using only the common interests of shared students. Doing so can frustrate teachers who, though they may be strengthening their cross-course instruction, miss opportunities to improve instructional strategies specific to their subject area. Judith Warren Little has found that "failing to attend systematically to the subject-specific aspects of teacher development and school reform seriously constrain[s] efforts to transform secondary schooling" (2002, 711). Math teachers who want to improve their practice need to be able to talk with math teachers even though they share no students, which, as we will see in Chapter 5, poses specific challenges for small-school faculties.

But how does a teacher in a large school develop collaborative relationships with colleagues when the structure and systems of the school impede, or ignore, the value of relationship-building? Steve Gardiner, a former Montana Teacher of the Year, writes about how he was able to create his own microprofessional learning community but had to do so essentially on his own:

> When I first came to the school I was just kind of looking around, listening to faculty meetings, listening on the announcements, for who was doing interesting projects. And then I just started making contact with those people, stopping by their classrooms to say "Hi; I'm a new teacher and I've got a similar interest to you," or "I've heard what you're doing and do you mind if I ask you some questions someday about what you're doing?"

And as soon as I started doing that things really changed, and I had professional relationships. I think it's certainly possible to have really strong professional relationships in the larger schools. There was that isolation for a while, the feeling that I am just not that significant here and that I could probably just disappear if I wanted to. Yet now, after 14 years, I don't feel that at all. I feel very much a part of the school.

Brian Greenberg, a former comprehensive high school English teacher in Los Angeles, speaks of a similar strategy, one that is dependent on the initiative of the individual teacher:

Some of the teachers who were trying to get better every day and really trying to have a different kind of relationship with the kids would meet for lunch once a week in one of our rooms. That was our refuge, where we could get together and really feel like we were kind of being pushed and supported for the reasons we all wanted to teach. I think finding a personal little small school within a school for yourself and those four or five or six teachers that really have those high expectations, care a lot about the kids, really want to get those great results—the other teachers really care about the kids and want good results, but there's a different level of commitment and buy-in— that can be a really good place to go for replenishment when the sea of mediocrity starts to get you down.

As both Steve and Brian demonstrate, it is possible for teachers to create their own professional relationships despite the large school's culture and systems that don't facilitate relationship-building and instead reinforce teacher isolation. All three of these teachers in comprehensive schools show how extraordinary teachers can create their own small networks in which teachers have relationships with each other that enable them to work collaboratively and grow professionally.

CONCLUSION

High school teachers need to move beyond the traditional conditions of school workplaces found in most large schools that continue to reinforce cultures of isolation, privacy, and protectiveness. They can do this by being in a school environment that values and facilitates relationships, shared interests, and constructive collaboration, which small schools are much more likely to offer. Alternatively, teachers in large schools can take the initiative and be persistent enough to carve out their own small professional community within a structure that was designed a century ago to work against it.

These examples of how small schools facilitate productive interactions among teachers have focused on how those interactions improve the quality of instruction in classrooms. But as will be explored in the next chapter, when teachers have an intimate knowledge of each other and their students, coupled with a culture of shared expectations and shared responsibility, the small school can alter the conventional role, authority, and identity of teachers, giving them a voice and responsibility not just for the students in their classrooms but for every student in the school, in every grade level, in every school space.

DISCUSSION QUESTIONS

1. When a team of teachers develops common classroom procedures, behavioral expectations for students, and common approaches to cross-discipline skills (such as writing), how does this inhibit teacher creativity? How does it promote it?

2. Think of a time recently when you collaborated with a colleague. What was the context? What were your shared interests, if any? Was it formal or informal? How do you think these factors affected the value of the conversation for you for improving student learning?

3. How might teachers' joint work foster more collaborative experiences among students in classrooms?

FURTHER READING

Coalition of Essential Schools (CES). 2009. CES National Web. http://www.essentialschools.org/.

Lortie, Dan C. 1975. *Schoolteacher: A Sociological Study.* Chicago: University of Chicago Press.

National School Reform Faculty. n.d. "NSRF Materials: Protocols." http://www.nsrfharmony.org/protocol/protocols.html.

Toch, Thomas. 2003. *High Schools on a Human Scale: How Small Schools Can Transform American Education.* Boston: Beacon Press.

CHAPTER FOUR

TEACHERS' VOICES AND ROLES IN SMALL SCHOOLS

- The Factory Model Role of Teachers

- The Value of Teachers' Voices in School Decisions

- Inevitable Interdependency in Small Schools

- Rewards and Challenges When Teachers Make Decisions

F ROM MY JOURNAL during my first year of teaching:

To be in our school's magnet program, you have to maintain a 3.0 grade point average. One big issue for me is how the students in the magnet program, predominantly white students, are in the AP and advanced classes, and almost everyone else, mostly African Americans from the school's surrounding neighborhoods, is in the regular or remedial classes. Even if you're a magnet student in a nonhonors class, your class is still composed primarily of magnet students. What really bothers me is that the teachers in the English department with me who I thought were pretty good turn out to be teachers of only magnet kids. Therefore, the weaker or less experienced teachers like me teach the kids with weaker skills, who theoretically should be getting the better and more experienced teachers because it seems more difficult to teach them.

Aside from the issue itself, I think what disturbs me is that no one seems to be talking about it, at least not openly. I'm not sure if that's because it has already been talked about and people have made their peace with it, or if it's because the topic is too sensitive and will ruffle feathers, or if it's because if people talk about it then we'll have to do something about it. I've talked about it with M—, but I'm not sure who else to talk to, or what to do about it. It's not as if I know all the different aspects (political, historical, educational) of the issue. How would the conversation even begin?

The issue of unequal representation in honors classes and inequitable resources for students along racial lines was as unacceptable for me twenty years ago as it is now. Was my voice as one teacher irrelevant in the school because it didn't feel invited, or did it not feel invited because it was irrelevant? I wasn't an authority on issues outside my classroom, so did I have any right to criticize the school? I'm sure other teachers felt the way I did, so how could we have connected, and toward what end? How could the school have created ways in which other teachers and I could get a broader perspective beyond my classroom and together, as a faculty, contribute to making our school better? If I did participate in improving the school outside of my classroom, could this make me a better teacher inside my classroom?

In the first chapter, we examined some key elements of the large comprehensive high school, primarily its emphasis on efficiency, and contrasted that with the small school's focus on relationships as the key to student success. In Chapter 2, we discussed how small schools, with fewer students, enable teachers to build relationships with and among their students to inform decisions about teaching and learning. Chapter 3 focused on the relationships among teachers and how small schools can create opportunities for teachers to share students, strategies, and ideas that build teachers' capacities and construct both an educationally coherent experience for students and a collaborative community of teacher learners. We now extend our scope beyond the relationships among students and teachers to the broader school environment and the organizational relationships among adults in small schools, particularly the relationships between teachers and site administrators (principal, vice principal) and the dynamics of decision-making. We will observe how the teacher's role, influence, and voice in a small school can be expanded and transformed, reflecting and determining the culture and context in which learning occurs for students.

THE FACTORY MODEL
ROLE OF TEACHERS

In the previous chapter we explored how teachers' work in traditional and large high schools isolates them from each other. In the traditional factory model, each teacher has a clearly defined responsibility for only those students she teaches during each period. When the class period ends and those students leave, the teacher becomes responsible for the entirely new set of students coming into the classroom. The movement of students from one teacher to the next has echoes of widgets constructed on an assembly line, with each teacher specializing to do certain kind of work "on" or "to" students for a certain amount of time, after which students move on to the next classroom. In this design of individualized and independent responsibility, the teacher is not expected to know or be responsible for students other than those she teaches during that particular period of instruction. In this model, teachers are given significant autonomy to make independent, isolated decisions for their students. As we saw in the last chapter, this can result in each teacher having entirely different approaches to teaching and learning, creating incoherence for students that undermines other teachers' decisions in their classrooms.

Above this inadvertent yet mutual undermining among teachers sits the administrator. Administrators in these kinds of schools may institute general guidelines for teachers (the course textbook, disciplinary policies, grading periods), but they generally defer most classroom-based decisions to the teacher and focus their attention on issues outside of the classroom. This traditional and enduringly typical division of labor can create efficiencies, particularly in a large school. If teachers are responsible for students in classrooms, administrators are responsible for students everywhere else and at all other times, such as when students are outside the classrooms (cafeteria, hallways) or during nonclassroom time (passing periods, before and after school).

In this separation of powers, if teachers are responsible for only their own students and are given the authority over what happens in classrooms, then the administrators, who become the only adults in the school who are responsible for all of the students, appropriately have the authority to make decisions that affect the entire school. As a teacher, I decide homework policies, instructional activities, and test content, and the administration manages assemblies, the master schedule, and fire drills. In this traditional and typical model of high school organizations, administrators and teachers assume different realms of decision-making, but this distribution of responsibilities and decisions does not make administrators and teachers complementary coequals, each with their own interlocking and respected domains; indeed, the demarcation of responsibilities is clearly hierarchical. Though principals have the authority to direct teachers to implement and enforce decisions that are not their own and directly affect the classroom (such as an attendance policy), teachers have little reciprocal ability to create policies that affect the entire school or the principal's work.

These separate and unequal realms of decision-making power create an uneasy tension in schools. Teachers are rarely needed, much less invited, to contribute meaningfully to schoolwide decisions, whether these decisions affect students and classrooms directly (behavior codes and scheduling) or indirectly (budgets, teacher assignments, hiring/firing). LaRavian Battle describes how in her previous work in a large comprehensive school, the administration had a top-down approach to its teachers:

> [At the large school] we had a department of maybe nineteen math teachers, and it was very top heavy. It was like, OK, the administration wants you to do this, this, this, this, and this. And that was it; we got our orders, and we went out, but there was never any room for 'What do you algebra teachers think?' There should have been, but there wasn't.

In most large high schools, and as LaRavian found in hers, an administrator provides information to teachers and expects that they will receive the information, understand it, and assimilate it into their practice immediately. Because teachers are often not included in conversations about schoolwide initiatives, but are asked to implement them, they can understandably become frustrated with their lack of influence.

Why is this dynamic more likely to occur in large schools? And how does teachers' isolation in many large high schools contribute to their lack of influence in decisions and therefore encourage and authorize administrators to lead from the top down?

In Chapter 3 we saw how teachers' isolation in large high schools often prevents them from building relationships with each other and can impede joint work. Because teachers in large schools are disconnected from the rest of their school and really experience only their own classrooms, they have a limited perspective on the school and are unable to meaningfully contribute to larger decisions, even if they want to and have the opportunity. Judith Warren Little explains: "The classroom overwhelms other sources of information. Individual preferences and prerogatives shape conclusions that might have been cast otherwise if informed by a more systematic and dispassionate comparison of practices and their consequences that reaches beyond classrooms. To the extent that successful decision making requires informed consideration of alternatives, teachers' general isolation places them at a disadvantage" (1990, 527). Teachers who are focused on and aware of only their own classroom experiences simply aren't in a position to make a decision that affects the entire school and their colleagues. It may actually be understandable in these circumstances for principals not to engage teachers in decision-making.

With limited understanding of the school beyond their classrooms, what teachers advocate for is based on their own perspective and priorities. Because it is difficult for an individual teacher to be heard and further her interests with so many other teachers, each with her own distinct and often incompatible interests, teachers gain power and voice when they band together around shared interests. One of the most accessible common interest groups in large high schools is subject departments (e.g., math, English), and because each department focuses only on its own curriculum, activities, and priorities, the departments compete against each other for resources and power. What results is what Hargreaves calls a "balkanization" of the school community: "Balkanization is characterized by strong and enduring boundaries between different parts of the organization, by personal identification with the domains these boundaries define, and by differences of power between one domain and another. It is an organizational pattern that sustains and is sustained by the prevailing hegemony of subject specialism . . . that restricts professional learning and educational change among communities of teachers" (1994, 235). The factory model endorsed the efficiencies of subject specialization, and the high school intentionally groups its faculty by content area. Departments compete with each other for the attention of the principal, vying for more classes in the school's course catalogue, more teachers on staff, or additional equipment and materials.

This internecine conflict pulls the school in many different directions, blurs any school focus, and impedes schoolwide progress.

In addition to the shared interests among teachers in departments, the teachers' union is designed to advocate for and protect teachers' interests—interests that include their working conditions and professionalism, due process protections, and compensation. The unions have historically provided teachers with important security and support, focusing primarily on ensuring that the administration adheres to the teacher's work contract. In my experience, the union rarely represents teachers' voices in school-specific decisions that don't implicate the teacher contract, such as pedagogy (whether the teachers are using advanced levels of Bloom's taxonomy in their questioning) or curriculum (whether the school's curricular theme should be the rainforest or civil rights). Teachers' voices are therefore invited in schools only as part of their subject department's interests or as represented by their union. In both cases, teacher voices attempt to influence the administrators' decisions; they are not part of the decision-making itself.

The exception to this is when a school has a site-based decision-making body, school cabinet, or parent-teacher association. In these governance models, representatives of the school constituencies, teachers among them, make decisions about certain schoolwide matters that can include budget or instructional initiatives. Yet as with all representative systems, these structures hear the actual voices of only a small number of teachers and don't ordinarily encourage, equip, or expect every teacher to become informed about and contribute directly to schoolwide decisions. Thus, despite this representative model of teacher voice, I haven't seen the governance model make teachers more informed about schoolwide considerations and their colleagues' perspectives. And sometimes, when a school has structures such as site-based decision-making, the administrators have little incentive to create or entertain additional avenues for teacher input; the place for teacher input exists at those meetings, so all teacher input must occur there. Needless to say, the agendas can become unwieldy and unfocused, which only further dilutes teachers' voices and amplifies the administration's power.

Even though schools may have these structures that intend to include teacher voices in decision-making, most teachers continue to be excluded from discussions about schoolwide issues and remain isolated from administrators and ignorant of broader perspectives of their school. Most administrators continue to make the majority of decisions and expect teachers to implement them consistently, which is not surprising, especially when the school is large. Considering how challenging it is to develop structures for meaningful conversations among teachers and then to organize systems in which teachers, with their limited perspectives and balkanized priorities, can contribute to schoolwide decisions, it too often simply becomes more efficient for the principal to make most of the decisions herself.

In this way the traditional position of teachers, still current in many large high schools, is to have little say or perspective about what happens outside their classroom, a continuing condition based on the factory model of teacher specialization and isolation. Schools therefore house coalitions of teachers who have similar interests (and who share similar limitations on their perspectives) that compete to get their interests addressed. Above the fray sits the administration, which makes decisions that affect teachers without meaningful contributions from them. The union and site-based representation bodies bring some teachers' voices to decision-making, but they are only a small step toward honoring all teachers in school decisions. To address how small schools are better equipped to engage teachers in decision-making, let's begin by stepping back and understanding why teacher voices are valuable in the first place.

THE VALUE OF TEACHERS' VOICES IN SCHOOL DECISIONS

One important benefit of including teachers in decisions that are beyond the day-to-day teaching and learning in their classrooms is very practical: to increase buy-in. When administrators mandate top-down policies in which teachers have not had meaningful input, each teacher mediates and translates those policies through her own systems of beliefs and priorities. Each teacher evaluates the applicability and appropriateness of those policies for her classroom context, modifying and sometimes ignoring the policies.

One day when I was an administrator, I announced a policy in which teachers were supposed to be outside their classroom doors during passing periods. Teachers weren't part of the decision; they were simply made aware of my expectations (after all, I felt, I was their supervisor). Yet it was a constant struggle to get consistent implementation across all classes. Some teachers disliked my policy because they didn't understand the rationale, disagreed with its purpose, or were discontented with how the decision was made; they rarely implemented the policy faithfully. The quality of policy implementation became a reflection of each individual teacher's level of support for that decision and a referendum on the level of confidence in the direction I was taking them. What this experience, as well as reactions to other decisions I made without their input, taught me was that a policy I might intend to bring coherence to our school environment through uniform application could, through teachers' uneven implementation, contribute instead to a fragmented environment for students—were they expected to act appropriately outside of classrooms if teachers were in the hallways in certain areas but not in others?—as well as stressful relationships among the adults—some wondered why they were standing outside classrooms monitoring hallways if other teachers weren't.

Stacie Pierpoint addresses the importance of involving teachers in schoolwide decisions:

> Teachers are more likely to buy into what they're doing and really believe in it if they actually have a say in its creation. That can be any part of the school, from assessments and curriculum, to what the school day looks like, to behavior management systems. Teachers want to be considered as professionals, and as part of the professional environment they would like their opinion valued. Ultimately at the end of the day it's the teachers that have to go in and teach and really want to go in and teach the students, so they value a chance to have input into how they're going to go about it.

She explains how engaging teachers to share their ideas and express their opinions gives them a sense of being valued as professionals, and including teachers' voices in decisions increases the fidelity of implementation. In addition, when teachers are part of decisions, they bring their expertise and knowledge of students to create more effective schoolwide policies. Better decisions can be made when more perspectives are considered; in particular, teachers' perspectives remind administrators of teachers' ongoing challenges and joys in the classroom, grounding administrators' thinking in the context in which the majority of the school community experiences the school. Finally, when teachers are invited to share perspectives on schoolwide issues, they gain a more expansive and complex view of their school. As we have learned, when teachers share students and speak about their experiences with other teachers, they become aware of what happens in other teachers' classrooms. When they are invited to be part of discussions with administrators and teachers with whom they don't share students, or who interact with their students outside the classroom context, they become less isolated, and their perspectives expand beyond classrooms to the hallways and the offices.

For example, when a small school faces budget cuts and teachers are invited to help make some critical decisions, they must look outside their own classroom needs and assess the implications for every aspect of the school. In the process of making these kinds of decisions, teachers gain opportunities to learn about the dynamics of the parent community, the budget, district and state pressures, and the master schedule construction, and they own the inevitably difficult decisions.

Of course, engaging parents, students, and the larger community in a school's decisions can engender buy-in and more investment in the decision. But because teachers are the ones primarily responsible for bringing the school's priorities and vision to the classroom, and considering their historically institutionalized isolation and exclusion from contributing to these priorities, it is particularly valuable to engage them in schoolwide decisions.

But in small schools, engaging teachers in decision-making is about more than getting buy-in. As we saw in Chapter 3, small schools, because they facilitate productive relationships among colleagues, can foster collaboration. Moreover, the fewer the teachers, the greater the impact each teacher's behavior has on every other teacher's, and student's, experiences. Therefore, in small schools, collaborative work with colleagues isn't an opportunity but an imperative on which the school's success rests. When there are fewer adults and students, there is *inevitable interdependency*: the success of each staff member is heavily affected by the actions of her colleagues, much more so than in a large school. In other words, regardless of whether an individual teacher wants to work closely with other teachers, or an administrator wants to include staff in decisions, in a small school neither has a choice.

INEVITABLE INTERDEPENDENCY IN SMALL SCHOOLS

Large schools, with thousands of students and dozens of classrooms, can ignore or "absorb" the outlier: the teacher who lets her students out a few minutes early or who doesn't enforce the no-text-messaging rule. The majority of teachers implement the school's policies and beliefs, and their students' experiences will be undisturbed. This is also true of the teacher outlier who goes above and beyond: one teacher's innovative teaching practices, higher expectations, or greater commitment, when the majority of teachers are less progressive or less committed, has little effect on other classrooms and the students schoolwide. In other words, individual actions are ripples in a very large pool.

In a small school, however, inconsistencies are magnified; when one teacher in a small school isn't implementing the same policies, all teachers are affected, particularly if they share students with that teacher. One teacher's failure to be on the same page as everyone else in the small school can weaken the school's overall effectiveness. This is true regarding issues of classroom management (a teacher who fails to implement all of the rules for behavior makes it more difficult for the other teachers to enforce them) and instruction (when one teacher teaches essays with different structures from what other teachers use, essay writing becomes more difficult for students and the other teachers). In a small school, "each one's teaching is everyone's business, and each one's success is everyone's responsibility" (Little 1990, 523). Teachers are inevitably interdependent.

Adults' interactions in small schools may be driven as much by everyone's individual self-interest in managing their inevitable interdependency as by a collective intent to create a professional learning community. It is not that teachers in small schools don't ever feel the desire to close their classroom doors and operate in their own isolated classroom; it is that they *can't work alone even if they want to*. First, when people are involved and invested in an idea, they implement it with more fidelity, so it becomes particularly important that teachers participate in decisions. Second, as explained in the previous chapter, when teachers share a group of students, each teacher can be more effective when every other teacher is giving the same message to students and implementing the same expectations in the same way. Therefore, small schools have a powerful incentive to engender teacher investment in decisions: if they exclude teachers from being involved in a decision, those teachers may not implement the decision, jeopardizing the schoolwide effectiveness of that decision's implementation, and everyone's job becomes more difficult.

A second implication for a small-school staff's inevitable interdependency is the teachers' roles and responsibilities. In the traditional school model, teachers specialize in teaching a subject area and are not generally expected, or asked, to assume administrative responsibilities; those remain within the domain of the administrator. Because small schools have many of the same nonteaching needs of large schools, but have fewer adults to manage those needs, responsibilities must be shared among the entire staff. There are often just too many administrative tasks to complete and too few administrators to do them. Michael Soguero describes how the demands of the small school create inevitable interdependency among a staff:

> Other than managing the masses [which a large school must do], almost every other facet of managing a school is still present in a small school. If I could make you a list of a hundred domains of concern in a school, they exist in a large or in a small school. However, in a small school, you have maybe no assistant principal to help the principal do it, so people have to rise and make that school successful and address some of those domains. It's not necessarily for some noble reason sometimes, [but] out of necessity: people just need to make sure they have supplies ordered or help the principal with the budget.

Small-school principals need teachers to assist with administrative tasks (such as ordering books), with managerial tasks (coordinating a field trip), and even with instructional leadership needs (helping to create a graduation assessment). When they take on administrative responsibilities, teachers gain a broader perspective and deeper understanding of the school, and this blended teacher/administrative distribution of responsibilities can flatten the organization and strengthen an interdependent community.

The principal shares her power by sharing administrative responsibilities. Not only does this give teachers opportunities to participate in administrative roles and gain perspectives from which they were previously excluded, but it also can give the principal permission to be more directly involved with supporting classroom instruction—the traditionally protected locus of teacher power. The teachers provide administrative support, so the principal benefits from teachers' administrative skills; similarly, the principal can provide instructional support, and the teachers benefit from the principal's classroom experience. The principal can even recast her role from supervisor of the teachers to facilitator of her teachers' learning, and with fewer adult "students" in the small school, the principal can become the teacher of the teachers and enjoy the benefits of a small "class size": more opportunities to know her teachers, to draw upon their strengths, and to differentiate her support. She can choose to model effective teaching for her teachers, engaging them in decisions, giving them choices and ownership over their work, allowing them to revise and improve their work, and differentiating her assistance.

Nevertheless, it can be difficult for a small school to strike the right balance between shared decision-making and appropriate delegation of authority. Despite the cooperative roles, most small schools still assign the principal the responsibility of evaluating teachers and the ultimate accountability for the school, just as in the large school. Yet small schools, unlike most comprehensive large schools, have the opportunity to create an adult culture in which teachers' voices are expected and considered, even when the principal reserves the power to make certain final decisions. Because of the small-school staff's inevitable interdependency, key schoolwide decisions simply cannot be made entirely by administrators with teachers being excluded or silenced—and realistically cannot be expected to benefit the school if they are. These characteristics are too often the norm in large schools.

But inviting teachers' voices and making decisions more collaboratively have many challenges.

REWARDS AND CHALLENGES
WHEN TEACHERS MAKE DECISIONS

As explained above, in small schools, teachers are expected to take on roles beyond classroom teaching and for which most teachers are unprepared—a stark contrast to the specialization expected of teachers in large schools. Supplies have to be purchased, meals served, phones answered, report cards printed and mailed, and the list goes on and on. Notice how both LaRavian Battle and Barbara Yeatman, a small-school curriculum facilitator in Humble, Texas, redefine themselves as a result of their expanded responsibilities:

> LaRavian: In the large school, I was a teacher. I talked to my parents, I talked to my students, occasionally I talked with the counselor, but that's all I had to do. I kept my door closed, and I handled whatever was happening in my classroom. The rest of the school was somebody else's problem and somebody else's job. . . . [The large school was restructured into separate small schools, and as] my department got smaller, as my student body got smaller, my job got bigger because I had to do so much with scheduling—helping with the master schedule, helping with the student schedule—even when we had to hire a teacher, I was on the interview

board. It's not just me as a teacher. They might need after-school tutoring; we had to make sure that if it's not
me [to provide it], then who?

BARBARA: You have to wear many, many, many hats. . . .
You can name at least twenty-five things that I do.
When you've got shared leadership, you're not only a
teacher, but maybe you're chairman of this committee
or you're in charge of something, and you have to be
willing to do many, many things—not just close your
door and teach English. I think that's very critical in a
small school. You have a small staff, you've got lots of
things to do, and the expectations there are very high.
The expectation is that you are going to be a very vital
cog in this wheel, and some teachers don't want that—
they really don't. But for me, the rewards are so great
when you end up in this kind of environment.

For LaRavian, her identity changed: "My job got bigger.
. . . It's not just me as a teacher," and in Barbara's school,
"You're not only a teacher." Both understand themselves,
with all their additional roles, as being something more
expansive, and less specialized, than the traditional definition of a teacher. With the opportunity to make decisions
that are normally not under a teacher's purview—to determine the school culture, the behavioral and academic
expectations for students, the daily, weekly, and yearly
schedule, or at minimum what curriculum to use and
how to collaborate with peers—and to take on additional
roles and responsibilities beyond the classroom, work in
small high schools can be exhilarating and overwhelming
simultaneously.

A second challenge of engaging teachers' voices in
small schools is that their staffs have to confront conflict,
something large schools can generally avoid. In many
large schools, when a teacher disagrees with a policy, she
has no clear venue in which she can express her opinion.

Because there are rarely mechanisms in large schools to allow for teachers' voices and discussions, a teacher who disagrees with a decision, usually made by administrators, is left to her own conscience to choose whether to implement the decision. Unless dissension is widespread or organized, a large-school community generally can ignore or "absorb" disagreements and dissent: if one teacher chooses not to follow the schoolwide policy that students are tardy if they are not in their seats when the bell rings, other teachers won't be affected, and the administration might not even be aware of her choice. Administrators in large schools may even expect uneven implementation by staff as an acceptable cost of efficient decision-making. The time and effort to create a meaningful structure for teachers' voices to be spoken and heard constructively is organizationally prohibitive, so it may in fact be preferable to accept inconsistency.

The difference in small schools is that though disagreement and dissent are just as present as in large schools, they are less hidden when there are fewer staff—not because people want to expose those disagreements but because they can't hide them. As we've seen, small schools require individuals to work less independently, to consider the effect of their actions on others, and to engage in conversations to negotiate common approaches and behaviors. In the course of these negotiations, staff's practices and beliefs about teaching and learning become less privatized and therefore reveal conflict. Little describes how, when there is increased sharing of ideas and honest dialogue, things will not run smoothly:

> Deeply held beliefs may be in conflict, with proponents of competing views each holding their own to serve the best interests of students. "Involvement" and "participation" [in school communities] require greater contact and visibility, greater awareness of one another's beliefs and practices, and greater reliance on verifiable information as a

basis for preferred action. In an effort to arrive at "deci-sions," teachers join discussions that sometimes link them to like-minded colleagues; those same discussions, how-ever, may force teachers to confront peers whose perspec-tives and practices they do not share or cannot admire. (1990, 521)

When teachers are asked to be part of decisions that af-fect the entire student body, disagreements among staff become more apparent and less avoidable. Conflict can be painful and add stress and exhaustion to an already demanding workplace. Yet, the process of resolving that conflict can yield a stronger, more resilient, trusting, and effective team of educators.

One small high school had a difficult time agreeing on the school's dress code. There was an expectation in the dis-cussion that the staff would come to an agreement, and as the conversation evolved, people exposed their deeper be-liefs implicated in this issue: freedom of expression, teach-ing students to be successful in the "culture of power," and the image of the school to visitors. Conflicting beliefs that had never been discussed caused tension among the staff that was only partially resolved by its decision—a decision all staff enforced with equal fidelity schoolwide.

Heather Cristol shares her experience of being part of a small school:

Like anything small, it's more like a family, so personali-ties are more magnified. It's like if you go to a small col-lege, and you break up with someone, but you're still going to see them at every meal. There's no escaping them. You can't just lose yourself in the anonymity of some large institution. If there's someone I don't get along with, sooner or later I'm going to have to share that person's classroom. I'm going to have to be on the same committee with them. You're all there together. You have to make it work.

The interdependency and shared responsibility in small schools invite, and compel, teachers to engage each other. Neither the compulsion nor the invitation exists to the same extent in large schools. There philosophical differences among teachers are rarely confronted because they are never aired, and the teaching community has no structures to establish relationships among one another to feel comfortable sharing, hearing, or addressing these differences. As uncomfortable as it may be, and as likely as it is to occur when people are open and honest, small-school teachers must be comfortable with conflict, confident that working through conflict builds a stronger community.

Another benefit of teachers working through conflict is that when adults become comfortable with and competent at addressing conflict in a community, they model for students how to address disagreements and build collaboration. When adults become experienced and proficient in shared decision-making, they can integrate that skill into their instruction, giving students the same kind of investment, responsibility, and accountability in their classes and their achievements that the teachers experience. For example, students can agree on classroom rules and can develop shared agreements about academic competency. They can collectively create rubrics that describe the characteristics of an effective presentation or define an exemplary group participant.

Being encouraged to contribute their voices to school-wide conversations also gives teachers a sense of power, a confidence that their opinion and ideas matter and that each individual can help the entire school improve. In a large school, because teachers are not generally invited to speak to schoolwide ideas, some simply endure each decision, resigned to powerlessness and fatalism: "That's just the way things are here." William Ayers and his coauthors call this condition "diminished imaginative space," a belief there can be no change and that no teacher's idea can make a difference (2000, 3). When teachers feel that their voice has no impact on the school's direction, they may cease considering possibilities. In small schools, when teachers are engaged and invested in decision-making, they can feel more actualized and creatively powerful. They realize that they can make a difference.

Involving teachers in decisions creates other challenges. Asking teachers to meaningfully participate in decision-making implies that they will need to invest resources and time that might otherwise be devoted to curriculum design and lesson planning. The priority of a school should be its instructional program, but involving teachers in decision-making can siphon them away from their classrooms. Some small schools carve out time in teachers' schedules to participate in schoolwide decisions; in other schools, they have essentially made a deliberate exchange of classroom instruction preparation for teachers' decision-making, confident that while teachers may have less time to plan their individual lessons, the time they invest in decisions that affect them will make their work easier and more successful.

An ironic challenge that some small schools face is that teachers may actually resist being involved in shared decision-making, even if they are directly affected by the result of those decisions. Teachers who have never been part of conversations about issues outside of their classroom may lack confidence that they can, and should, make informed choices that have an impact on students outside their classroom, particularly if they affect what goes on in their colleagues' classrooms. Teachers also may be hesitant to be involved in schoolwide decision-making because to do so is to accept a shared responsibility for all students, not just the students they teach. This role asks teachers to make a fundamental and, to many of them, frightening leap in ownership and accountability, which can overwhelm a teacher used to having control over only those students in her classroom and being exempt from thinking about other students.

Another challenge of shared decision-making in small schools is that too much cohesion in a small group of people can actually harm their effectiveness. When everyone is invested in a set of ideas, it is a fine line between common agreements and cultish adherence. Some small schools have such deeply ingrained convictions among their staff and take such pains to limit conflicting perspectives in their staffing choices that they can become as unaware of alternatives as the teacher who is isolated in her classroom.

And perhaps the most important caution of all is that shared decision-making is the means to an end, not the end itself. A small school can leverage its small number of adults and the relationships among them to develop the optimal way to make the best decisions; most small schools believe it is through some kind of democratic process. But as Nancy Mohr writes: "If democracy means everyone gets to vote on everything, endlessly, instead of everyone working for the inclusion of all voices and ideas, then it will become an albatross instead of a road toward greater justice and equity. Equitable decision-making has to be focused not on the right to make the decision but on making the right decision" (2000, 148).

Some small-school staffs, because of their desire for agreement, become more concerned with consensus than with doing the right thing. Authentic conversations within a supportive environment can lead to decisions that may not be in the best interests of all students, that serve instead to perpetuate inequities and deny opportunities. In the most successful small schools, the decision-making process always shapes, and the decisions are measured by, larger principles of equity and a dedication to creating a learning environment in which every student can succeed.

CONCLUSION

Involving teachers' voices in decisions helps to build a school culture that values transparency, meaningful interactions, acceptance of conflict, and shared ownership of actions and their consequences. In a small school, the staff's inevitable interdependency necessitates teachers' participation in decision-making and responsibilities outside the classroom. If we want students to learn these important skills, the adults must learn them first. When teachers experience sharing ideas and working together to resolve conflicts and make decisions—an opportunity that is much more likely in small schools—they change the way their classrooms operate and allow students to experience shared decision-making and conflict resolution, critical skills for success in the adult world. Similarly, when teachers experience being active, powerful co-owners of the entire school with voices that are heard, they can create classrooms and schools that listen to and respond to student voices as well.

In a large school, there are options for teachers to get involved in the existing representative structures, including the union, and to influence those bodies to discuss teaching and learning issues. Additionally, when teachers can be involved in hiring, they can help to get like-minded colleagues on the faculty. An emerging theme throughout the first four chapters of this book is that in order for teachers in large schools to adopt some of the effective strategies that small schools facilitate, the large school needs to adopt smallness: a classroom in which the teacher gets to know her students well or a department in which teachers know each other and share lessons. Both of these examples of smallness depended upon the initiatives of visionary individual teachers. In Chapter 5, we will explore how large schools, particularly in recent years, have recognized the valuable principles behind small schools and sought to reorganize themselves to facilitate the powerful opportunities in small learning environments. But can large schools really become small?

DISCUSSION QUESTIONS

1. How does a school balance voice with authority? In what matters should teachers have equal power? In what matters should they not? How would a school decide?

2. Teachers need time and support to build the skills needed to make good schoolwide decisions, and principals need time and support to build the skills necessary to involve others in decisions. How can each group build those skills?

3. What implications do the interdependency and transparency of practice in small schools have for how teachers are assessed? How, if at all, should teachers' voices play a role in employment decisions?

4. Some argue that new teachers should not teach in small schools because in addition to the shared work with colleagues, extra teaching responsibilities, and participation in shared decision-making, the teacher has to learn to teach. Others believe that small schools, because of the collaborative relationships among colleagues, are ideal for new teachers. What do you think?

FURTHER READING

Darling-Hammond, Linda. 1997. *The Right to Learn: A Blueprint for Creating Schools That Work.* Jossey-Bass Education Series. San Francisco: Jossey-Bass.

Dufour, Richard, and Robert Eaker. 1998. *Professional Communities at Work: Best Practices for Enhancing Student Achievement.* Alexandria, VA: Association for Supervision and Curriculum Development.

Senge, Peter, et al. 2000. *Schools That Learn: A Fifth Discipline Fieldbook for Educators, Parents, and Everyone Who Cares about Education.* New York: Doubleday.

• Trying to Be Everything— and Its Costs

• Smallness and Fragility

• Taking Smallness for Granted

• Communicating with Others About Small Schools

• Some Additional Considerations for Small Schools

• Large Schools and Smallness

CHAPTER FIVE

CHALLENGES FOR TEACHERS IN SMALL SCHOOLS, OPPORTUNITIES FOR TEACHERS IN LARGE SCHOOLS

FROM MY JOURNAL during my first year of teaching:

Every year the magnet program runs a "Character Day." Weeks ahead, each student chooses a character from a novel, researches the person, and writes a monologue for that character. On Character Day, each student dresses up as that character and, having memorized their monologue, acts it out for English class. It's pretty neat to see all of the magnet students dress up on the same day and give these presentations. They and their teachers really get into it. Although in the past the activity has been only in the magnet program, this year we tried to have all students schoolwide participate. The magnet program teachers explained the concept to other teachers in a staff meeting and circulated some handouts. I got to know one of the teachers who teaches in the magnet program, so she gave me some additional help so I could prepare my classes to do it.

Expanding the activity schoolwide seemed like a good idea, and helped make the educational activities more available to all students. What happened today was that only a small portion of teachers outside the magnet program did it. I guess some teachers didn't really buy into it, or maybe they just didn't understand what it was or how to do it well. Is it better to have some activity done well among a few teachers and their students than done schoolwide but not consistently for all students? Would having the nonmagnet students do their own activity fuel an "us-versus-them" mentality, or would it be okay, and maybe good, if different groups of students had different experiences?

Clearly, having a unique program within the school raised concerns for me, in part because I was envious of what those students and teachers were experiencing. The teachers worked closely with each other and created interesting program-wide activities and a culture that got kids excited about learning. I wondered if it was even possible to have such an activity schoolwide, or if it could only be implemented well among smaller groups of teachers and students. Was there something special, and even desirable, about having smaller groups of teachers and students be clustered together?

So far we have explored the opportunities that small schools can provide for teachers in their individual classes, across classes, and with colleagues, and previous chapters described some common challenges for teachers in small schools, such as confusing hugs for calculus, managing multiple responsibilities outside the classroom, and living with conflict. This chapter first addresses some additional cautionary dynamics that are specific to (and perhaps unavoidable in) small schools, and I then expand on a theme woven throughout the first four chapters: to what extent can a large high school, and teachers within it, adopt practices that are common in small schools?

TRYING TO BE EVERYTHING— AND ITS COSTS

One challenge faced by many small schools is the need to negotiate not being large. It seems obvious that small schools can't be large schools—they have smaller facilities, less money, fewer staff, and a structure that supports a different focus and purpose. Nevertheless, the students, even if there are fewer of them, will have the same range of interests and needs as students in a large school. There will be students who are English learners, are from low socioeconomic backgrounds, have learning and emotional disabilities, want advanced challenges, and have particular hobbies, interests, and talents. The staff of a small school often feels pressure to expand and meet all of the demands of the students and families, to offer more choices and activities—in other words, to be like a large school. But unlike in a large school, in the small school a limited number of adults are available to meet these needs and interests. They often struggle to assemble staff with a sufficient range of expertise to meet the needs of all students, even when they may be legally required to meet certain students' needs (special education, English learners). The school must make hard choices about how to allocate its limited financial and personnel resources.

Let's separate the variety that large schools offer into two categories:

- The "horizontal curriculum"—the range of courses offered, including the extracurricular activities
- The "vertical curriculum"—the different levels of a single course

In terms of horizontal curriculum, small schools clearly cannot offer the vast array of foreign languages, core electives (e.g., journalism), or arts courses that large schools can. Nor do they usually have the resources to support the wide range of after-school activities present in large high schools. To compensate for the school's limited personnel and resources, some schools form partnerships with community organizations, postsecondary institutions, third-party providers, or businesses to provide opportunities that large schools have. A small school may pay for an adjunct teacher from a community college to teach a forensics class, a parent may volunteer to teach conversational Japanese, a local Boys and Girls Club may supply a coach for the school's basketball team, or an art center may offer its facility to a group of students to use after school. Even when they form partnerships to provide services, small schools still limit options for students.

A small school's staff, because of the school's limited resources and fewer personnel, must find ways to offer their students scaled-down versions that capture the essence of traditional high school rituals so that the school is a "real school" in the eyes of students. Dances may be in the school's common or multipurpose space, sports competitions may be intramural in tone, and concerts might be by students' own bands. Some small schools organize leagues to cohost events and organize interschool competitions. When several small schools share a larger facility, they may develop building-wide teams to compete as a single large school.

To some students, families, and faculty, not having the options available in large comprehensive schools disqualifies the small school from being a good fit despite its other benefits, the assumption being that the fewer school options and activities, the weaker the student participation will be. In fact, small high schools have a higher rate of student participation in activities even though the schools offer fewer of those activities (Coladarci and Cobb 1996). Crosnoe and his coauthors (2004) found, using evidence from nearly 15,000 students in eighty-four schools, that increases in school size were associated with *decreases* in extracurricular participation. One explanation may be that because many activities have a fixed number of possible participants, a smaller proportion of students have the opportunity to be a participant (e.g., the basketball team can have only five players on the court regardless of the school's size). An alternate hypothesis is that because larger schools have been found to have a weaker interpersonal climate than small schools (Crosnoe et al. 2004), perhaps the students in a large school are less invested in the school's nonrequired opportunities.

In a small school, the vertical curriculum is similarly limited. There aren't enough students, or teachers, to warrant multiple levels of academic subjects, so there is usually only a single English course that all ninth-grade students take, not separate remedial, regular, and honors English. In contrast to the large high school's varied academic expectations for students (both remedial English and honors English satisfy the school's ninth-grade English requirement), a small school sets the same academic expectation for all students. Whether because of the school's values or because it has no other practical choice, having the same academic expectation for all students promotes greater academic equity. As Lee and Smith found, "high schools with constrained curricula, in which all students take a similar set of course offerings, appear to increase the learning of all of their students" (1995, 258).

When the small school offers a foreign language, or a fourth year of mathematics, no student can opt out of taking it and enroll in a less academically rigorous course because there isn't another class offered. In fact, a small school has few actual "electives"; rather, courses that in the large high school are considered elective are part of the small school's core academic program, required of all students. Additionally, research has shown that there is no relationship between school size and curriculum quality (e.g., Fowler and Walberg 1991; Monk and Haller 1993), and for all the additional courses that large schools can offer, it has been found that the expanded curriculum in larger schools tends to be composed not of higher-level courses in core subjects but of additional introductory courses in noncore areas (McGuire 1989), which does little to increase student achievement. It is the wide range of courses in comprehensive high schools that actually facilitates tracking and academic stratification. As Leithwood and Jantzi summarized their review of empirical evidence about school size effects, "Breadth of curriculum is no longer a justification for large schools. . . . It is now regarded as a threat to the academic progress of most students" (2009, 484).

But families, students, and even teachers can have a difficult time dismissing the appeal of the range of options that large schools offer. One way that some small schools approach the issue of variety and choice for students is to reframe where important choices occur in the school. *Large comprehensive high schools have many elective choices and tracks of core classes, but there is little student choice within each class; with so many students in teachers' classes or loads, all students within each class must do the same activities and be evaluated in the same way. In the small school, choice is within the classroom instead of outside it.* As explained in Chapter 2, teachers with fewer students and deep knowledge of them can differentiate instruction and provide a variety of assessment options, so students within a classroom can have distinct, and student-determined, learning experiences. Even if they have fewer noncore subject choices, students can be offered multiple ways to connect with a subject and excel in each course. An alternative way small schools frame their program is the following: there are fewer choices in high school so students have more choices *after* high school.

Focus point

For example, in Stacie Pierpoint's small school, all students were required to take her Spanish class as their foreign language; they had no choice. Yet she offered students lots of choice within her required class:

> I try as much as possible to work choice into the assignments so that students might find something that they are interested in and have some way to complete it. The

choice could be on a topic or the type of assignment. [For example, it] could be a multimedia project; it could be a skit; it could be a combination of emails that they write out. It would depend on the specific project, but it might be a cartoon or a mini graphic novel—something that could tap into the interest or the skills of the students of the class. Choice goes with everything.

Stacie's ability to differentiate her instruction, in part because in a small school she was able to identify students' interests and strengths, may have done more to engage students and support their success than some large high school's multiple language classes, which often require students to demonstrate their understanding in a single, teacher-defined way.

The bottom line, nevertheless, is that the small school has to admit that it can't meet every student's interests and needs, a concession that can be hard to reconcile with the overarching commitment of educators to serve every student. Stacie explains, "We may think we have a better education setup academically, but we lose some students because, for example, we don't have the space for the football teams or those types of things. . . . It has been a struggle." The struggle for many small schools' staffs becomes, therefore, to convince parents and students that the sacrifices the school staff accepts—fewer electives, fewer clubs, and fewer students—are worth the benefits: personalization, safety, and academic success. Many parents and students have difficulty understanding small high schools, especially when they don't have the typical characteristics of high schools they have experienced or witnessed: crowded hallways, Friday night football games in large venues, lavish proms, and large musical and theatrical productions. If parents attended large high schools, and as depersonalizing as it may have been, they often romanticize their experience and want it for their children.

When faced with the pressures to become large, successful small schools recast their limited course offerings as a strength and implement a constrained academic curriculum embedded with high expectations and differentiated instructional opportunities for every student.

Nevertheless, even when the small school strikes a thoughtful balance between academic constraints and elective options, the pressure on teachers is significant. In addition to teachers having many other responsibilities in the school (see Chapter 4), because there aren't enough students to enable teachers to teach only one or two courses (or "preps") each day, it is not unusual for each teacher to teach many different courses in a single year, which may include courses in their subject area, an elective, and an advisory class. Teaching multiple courses helps students make connections among different academic experiences and helps deepen student-teacher relationships, but having more preps places significant strain on teachers, especially new teachers who are learning to teach several new courses simultaneously. A related challenge is that it may be that no two colleagues within a small high school teach the same course; for example, there might be only one teacher who teaches ninth-grade English. For this reason, teachers in small schools can struggle to get subject-area support. In a large school, by contrast, a teacher has many colleagues who teach in his or her content area, and likely the same course, so there are plenty of perspectives, experiences, and resources to share. Inasmuch as teachers in small schools have the ability and incentive to work collaboratively to benefit their shared students, they often struggle to establish meaningful collaboration related to shared content.

LaRavian experienced this within the demands of the math course offerings: "The math department in my [small] school is three math teachers, and we're teaching everything from algebra with an algebra assistance class through calculus, so we're splitting these subjects between the three of us. I teach three preps, the other two teachers teach two preps each, and none of us are teaching the same subject, so it kind of inhibits collaboration."

Judith Warren Little has found that schools that subordinate subject-specific teacher learning—and instead promote teachers as generalists who focus on "the art of teaching" independent of content—lose opportunities for professional development and for advancing the school's vision (2002, 701). Many small schools have difficulty avoiding this pitfall because they have fewer faculty (few teachers teach the same course) and because they are organized in interdisciplinary teams who share students. Teachers in small schools must therefore go outside of their school to receive content-area support through informal relationships with other colleagues or, if they are fortunate, through formal networks with teachers at other schools. Yet when a small school's needs seem all-consuming, it can be difficult to make these content-specific connections with teachers outside the school and even more challenging to find the time to communicate meaningfully with those other teachers.

Trying to be, if not everything, then as much as possible, combined with the responsibilities and roles teachers in small schools are asked and able to have outside the classroom, can take a toll on a teacher's psychological, emotional, intellectual, and physical energy. It can be difficult to sustain enthusiasm and commitment to the work of small schools when there are so many challenges and responsibilities.

Stacy Spector explains, "In order to get to sustainability and traction, with everybody knowing what everybody's doing and thinking and valuing and providing evidence of student learning, it comes with great energy and great costs, mentally, emotionally, and physically. To avoid burnout, it's important to figure out how to keep everyone charged and focused on the work and to celebrate, to acknowledge that this is the most difficult, yet most challenging, work that anyone anywhere can engage in." As she articulates so well, adults in small schools must find ways to use their limited energy wisely, to preserve and protect their commitment and drive. Because the environment, dynamics, and teaching and learning experiences are unique to each small school, teachers can feel isolated from the larger community of educators. Organizations for small schools, such as the Coalition of Essential Schools and the Center for Collaborative Education Small School Network, and additional organizations for charter schools (most of which are small) are established to help teachers learn about other small schools' work and experiences.

TEXTBOX 5.1   CENTER FOR COLLABORATIVE EDUCATION (CCE) SMALL SCHOOLS NETWORK

CCE Small Schools Network was established through a grant from the Bill and Melinda Gates Foundation to "demonstrate the power of small schools" and to help others to consider and design small schools. Their resources include the publication *Creating Small Schools: A Handbook for Raising Equity and Achievement* (French et al. 2007) and a planning guide. For more information see http://www .nessn.org.

SMALLNESS AND FRAGILITY

A second challenge related to the small school's identity is its fragility.

As explained briefly in Chapter 4, in a large comprehensive high school, events can occur and be ignored, never really disrupting the school. Fights occur in one area of the campus, and adults and students elsewhere on campus don't even know about it; a weak teacher whose students cause classroom disruptions can be ignored by her colleagues. The egg-carton isolation in which teachers operate generally insulates them from hearing about, much less being affected by, problems elsewhere in the school.

In small schools, on the other hand, events that normally could be ignored are felt throughout the school, in what Nancy Mohr describes as an "amplified impact" (2000, 143). I have experienced how a fight in one part of a small school is felt everywhere: with fewer students, everyone in the school—students and adults—likely knows the students involved, and the whole school focuses on the welfare of the students, possible disciplinary consequences, and the impact on the rest of the school community. The tone in the entire school is altered. Another example is when students are having behavior problems in one teacher's class in a small school: it affects every other teacher—as shown in Chapter 3, every teacher's job becomes more difficult when one teacher struggles—and the rest of the adults may have little choice but to respond to the issue through discussions with students and support of the teacher. A single event or teacher can affect and even damage the whole school community's stability and identity. For example, in one small school I visited, a disgruntled employee was able to sabotage the rest of the staff's efforts by undermining their collective agreements about student expectations. The school became consumed with mitigating the teacher's influence and reinforcing behavioral expectations, and the school community lost its academic focus.

A less extreme but perhaps more profound example of a small school's fragility is when a vocal minority of teachers moves the school in a direction contrary to the school's mission. Michael Soguero describes one situation:

> Small schools tend to be more sure of what they're standing for, like if they decide to have a particular approach or they decide to have a theme. Those things, hopefully, are not negotiable. When they're all negotiable, then I think they're bad small schools. You start a school for the environment, and then people say, "Well, I don't like that idea anymore. Let's do something else." [One particular school] is an example. In it you studied the city's infrastructure, which was the basis of the school's curriculum, and then that school, unfortunately, allowed

for people to have different opinions about that instructional focus when it was the foundation for the school.

Focus point

Michael had worked in a small school that had its vision derailed by one or two teachers in the name of inclusive decision-making. *Hearing all voices is not the same as accommodating everyone's opinion, and involving everyone in decision-making is not the same as requiring consensus; small schools can find themselves in procedural tar pits when they try to get everyone to agree.* Not only do small schools need to define their nonnegotiables and make them truly sacrosanct, but they also need to clearly define their decision-making process to ensure that voices are heard, decisions can be made, and certain core beliefs will not be reconsidered.

TAKING SMALLNESS FOR GRANTED

As Chapters 2 and 3 described, because small schools so easily facilitate relationships, educators can falsely believe that relationships alone are sufficient to create an effective learning environment. Although knowing students and caring for them can yield a "bump" in student achievement, especially compared with impersonal comprehensive schools, some teachers in small schools rest on those relationships and "confuse hugs for calculus" (Fine 2005, 11).

When teachers' relationships with students are an end, and not a means, for effective teaching and learning, teachers no longer intentionally leverage the school's smallness. As Josh Anderson, a former Kansas Teacher of the Year, found while visiting schools throughout the state, small schools sometimes take smallness for granted:

> Professional relationships between teachers and students cannot be formed accidentally. They must be built into the structure and daily operations of the school. It cannot be a one-day topic for staff development, and it cannot be outsourced to the teacher through inspiring or sad stories.

Instead, it must be initiated and supported by a systematic network of opportunities, interventions, and consequences that all adults are expected to use and support. Smaller communities perceive themselves to be more caring and more thoughtful than the bigger communities, but these perceptions don't always match reality. . . . [A difference between large schools and small schools is] the perceived need to adopt a formal structure to improve student-teacher relationships, and it is the smaller schools that think they need them the least, which might make them more vulnerable to failure.

Josh identifies how some small-school staffs can fool themselves into believing that their student-teacher relationships don't require structure and explicitness, when, in fact, systems and structures for student learning, like the protocols for teacher collaboration, are how teachers construct relationships with their students.

For example, the teacher in a small school who believes she can establish relationships with students simply by being friendly and compassionate misses the point of relationships. In this case, students' experiences in classrooms and the academic expectations placed on them become dependent on teachers' personalities and individual styles. Instead, when a teacher plans deliberate ways to build relationships, she can learn information about her students that will aid her ability to teach each one. One example of an intentional structure to build teacher-student relationships is advisories (see Resource C). A school might also establish a schoolwide instructional culture of writing, in which every class expects students to write each day. Teachers can assess student thinking and learning daily, share students' writing with each other, and develop a deeper understanding of students' needs to serve them more effectively. When teachers articulate, refine, and codify procedures and structures for interactions between students and teachers, and among teachers, they fully leverage smallness.

COMMUNICATING WITH
OTHERS ABOUT SMALL SCHOOLS

Small high schools, despite their proliferation in some
major cities (for example, New York, Boston, Chicago,
Oakland), are still relatively unfamiliar to many students
and adults. For this reason, teachers in small schools find
themselves frequently explaining their small school.
Many students entering high school and their parents
know only the comprehensive high school model for secondary education. In addition, teachers in small schools
may find themselves introducing the concept of a small
school to two other constituencies: community organizations and teachers.

As explained previously, most small schools don't have
the funds or facilities to provide health services, state-of-
the-art science equipment, and recreation or performance spaces—important aspects for students' academic
and social development—so some small-school staffs
turn to community businesses and institutions. These organizations may have little familiarity with a small
school, but I have found that businesses and organizations are interested in working with small schools; they
see similarities between the size of the school and their
own size, or they appreciate the school's personalized student-centered approach. In one more example of small
schools' capacity and priority to personalize relationships, businesses and other organizations can experience
a quality of partnership that happens less often in large
schools. In a study of Chicago's small schools, Patricia
Wasley and her colleagues found characteristics of the relationship between small schools and external partners
that should by now sound familiar:

> A number of the [external] partners have in the past col-
> laborated with larger, more conventional schools, in ad-
> dition to the small schools. When asked about the
> difference, they uniformly acknowledged a difference

and a preference for working with small schools. Across the board they indicated that in these small, more intimate settings, partners got to know more than one person in a school; they were asked for more than the conventional requests for money or fundraising; they were included in planning and assessment of the small school's progress; they experienced an internal sense of accountability by educators for the youth; and they agreed to participate in long-term (often five-year) relations with schools. They felt more engaged; they saw the consequences of their engagement and, in turn, were confident to become advocates for a more rigorous public education system. (Wasley et al. 2000, 56)

Wasley found that external organizations, by partnering with small schools, became more informed about and engaged in public education. In an era when public schools need all the advocates they can get, this is an important by-product.

Another, perhaps unanticipated, constituency that teachers in small high schools may find themselves educating are their teacher colleagues in large high schools. Small high schools, at least public ones, are a relatively new phenomenon, and secondary teachers who aren't in small schools likely have preconceptions about them, including the working conditions, whom they serve, and their impact on large schools. Small schools can hold a mirror up to large schools and provide a context for teachers to reexamine their practice and redefine teaching and learning. When teachers share with other teachers their experiences in small schools, it exposes other teachers to a different model of their work. Why do teachers share students? What do teachers talk about together, and how do they talk with each other? Why are teachers more transparent about their practice? How do teachers build relationships with students, and why? How do students demonstrate success? Teachers who may not normally consider these issues in their large-school context might be interested to learn how some teachers do things in their small-school context, and they may begin to imagine how they might incorporate smallness into their large school. It's an opportunity to speak with other professionals about the day-to-day activities as well as the philosophical orientation and purpose of the work—how a small school's understanding of how students learn and their goals for students fundamentally alter how teachers interact with students and with each other.

With every constituency, whether it be families, students, outside organizations, or other teachers, when teachers of small schools talk about their experience, they aren't just describing how a high school can be small; they're explaining *what a high school can become when it is small.*

SOME ADDITIONAL CONSIDERATIONS FOR SMALL SCHOOLS

In addition to these considerations for small-school teachers and, to a more limited extent, for teachers in large schools contemplating smallness, several critical issues in small schools remain unresolved:

- Teachers in small schools are expected to assume many additional responsibilities beyond teaching in their classrooms. Should this condition change their compensation model?
- Although small schools have the opportunity to use shared decision-making, the school leader significantly affects the school's vision, agenda, and tone in the school. How dependent, ultimately, is the small school on its school leader, and what implications does this have for how the school can ensure staying power and stamina?
- Many small high schools serve students of color but are led and staffed by white people. How does this affect the culture of the school and the

process for teaching and learning? How does this affect voice and ownership? That is, whose school is it? What issues of equity might this raise?

- Small schools depend on a coherent and cohesive community of adults and students. How can this emphasis potentially exclude ideas that could cause conflict as well as enhance the community? Could coherence exclude particular groups of students and teachers?

These thorny issues implicate some of the crucial purposes and dynamics of public education, in both large and small high schools. As Chapter 4 discussed, difficult issues rise more quickly to the surface in small schools than in large schools, where deeper questions of purpose are normally unaddressed. Especially when one is considering employment in a small school, coming to terms with these questions in your own mind will enable you to solidify your beliefs and make you a more educated job applicant. For teachers in large schools considering smallness, reflecting on these questions and the other issues listed above will help you to clarify your purpose for smallness and be more strategic with implementing it.

LARGE SCHOOLS AND SMALLNESS

Paul Cain succinctly explains the fundamental challenge of large schools:

> You've got a school of 1,800 to 1,900 kids, and kids can get lost. Kids can pass from class to class, day in and day out, and never be called on, never be asked anything—they're just sitting there, filling out papers. And while some kids think that's what they want, I really believe that kids want to be seen and not just be part of the scenery. If you don't make a concerted effort, you're going to overlook some of those kids, and we can't afford

to. All they need is a little bit of attention to get them
fired up.

Paul confirms that students need adults to pay attention
to them, "to be seen and not just be part of the scenery."
Throughout this book, we've analyzed how a teacher's relationships with students and colleagues are qualitatively
different when the school is small, but perhaps it is more
accurate to say, "when the school has qualities of smallness." Because the research is nearly incontrovertible that
smallness improves learning opportunities for students
and teaching possibilities for adults, many comprehensive
high schools try to capture elements of smallness—to
change the *experienced* size of their school, if not the actual size. For the teacher who is exploring different school
models, or who is in a large school but wants to provide
students with some of the important aspects of small
schools, what are ways practitioners bring smallness to a
large school environment?

In Chapter 2, we saw how teachers can create smallness in their classrooms by building a classroom culture
that personalizes relationships. Like the exemplary teachers in large high schools, an individual teacher in a comprehensive school can try to make her classroom "small"
by getting to know about students' lives outside of class,
tapping into their interests, having rules and expectations
that enable students to play more participatory roles in
the classroom, or even explicitly tracking interactions to
make sure that she talks to each student periodically.
Brian Greenberg, a former teacher in a comprehensive
high school in Los Angeles, explains the culture of his
classroom:

> I used to give a speech to my students when I was in a
> comprehensive high school and said, "Whatever you've
> done in your past, whatever you do all day long, what-
> ever you do when you're not in school, that's your busi-
> ness. But when you walk in *this* door, this is where you

bring your best self, and this is where you rise to a higher level of expectation than you've ever put on yourself before." You can do it effectively in a classroom. That level of knowing your kids, having that intimacy, having that personal relationship, can be done in a comprehensive high school. It's just hard because rather than having six teachers doing that all day long for every kid, you're the one part of the day that's that way for them. The potential benefit of that would be that you can stand out even more by distinction, because if other teachers aren't doing these tasks, you could really make your class look and feel very different.

Brian brought smallness to his classroom by contrasting his learning environment with the largeness outside his door—whether that was the school or the outside environment. For him, it was both difficult and empowering to create this isolated island of smallness.

In Chapter 3, we saw how teachers in large schools can build informal networks with like-minded peers within the large school to construct a support system, a sounding board, and a learning community.

STEVE GARDINER: When I came [to the large school] one day I had a technology question and I walked into the technology teacher's room. I started asking him some questions and he was really friendly and really helpful. Pretty soon I was back there with another question and then another one. And one day I stopped by and said, "Hey, I've got a bunch of things to talk about. Do you mind if I just bring my lunch and we sit and talk"? And we've had lunch together for 10 years now. We've talked about every subject imaginable inside education and outside education. The information is out there, and the experience is out there, so why not tap into it?

To Steve, teaching in a comprehensive school, it was up to him to establish relationships with colleagues, to "tap into" the wealth of experience and knowledge of his large school's teaching staff. Even though the large school does not usually facilitate collegial relationships, teachers can create them on their own. The question remains, however, whether those teacher relationships can yield the same quality of professional growth without institutional structures and supports.

To provide institutional support, some large comprehensive schools attempt to create smallness in their overall structure, hoping to capitalize on the strengths of largeness—the variety of courses, the competitive extracurriculars, the facilities, and the efficiencies—but at the same time to implement designs that personalize students' learning and foster professional relationships among adults. Often these occur in the form of "houses," "academies," or "schools within a school" that cluster a set of teachers with a group of students and often have their own theme or academic focus. Commonly called a small learning community (SLC), this design would seem in theory to provide students and teachers the best of both worlds. In practice it is challenging for schools to implement this model successfully. The SLC's smallness is often insufficiently insulated from the large school, and it can become a constant battle for the SLC's staff and students to withstand the pressures of the large school's culture, to preserve its own identity, and to fully exploit the opportunities of smallness. Although the SLC's teachers intend to establish norms and expectations distinct from the large school's, what often ends up happening is that the actions and experiences of the SLC's teachers and students revert to those of the comprehensive school.

Why, in many cases, can't the SLC preserve its own culture, beliefs, and expectations? First, resource limitations and decisions about the interface between the SLC and the rest of the school can make the conceptual walls of the SLC "porous": teachers within an SLC may teach students outside the SLC, or the SLC's students are allowed to take (or are assigned to) classes taught by teachers outside the SLC. When this happens, the SLC's teachers no longer share the same group of students, and they must spend more time competing against the large school's culture and reinforcing their own with the students who attend classes in both contexts. Additionally, the classrooms of the SLC's teachers may be dispersed throughout the large-school facility rather than being clustered. Under these circumstances, it becomes more difficult for the SLC teachers to build relationships, work collaboratively to meet the needs of shared students, and engage in authentic joint work. The teachers' and students' experiences revert to those of the larger comprehensive school. According to Peter Ross, to make an SLC work as intended,

> there need to be enough boundaries around the way the adults work with each other and around the students they have so that you can get positive outcomes. For instance if you have a structure where you're only sharing your kids 30–40% of the time, you're kind of wasting your time. You might get a little bit of bump in terms of personalization, but you're not going to get all those other things. There isn't any exact tipping point, but there has to be enough in place where the adults have enough ownership of the community and the students are sufficiently spending enough time in whatever the core is, so that you really have some identity, and you can actually get to that rigorous place.

The second and more critical challenge with SLC implementation is to ensure that the SLC has "sufficient separateness and autonomy to permit staff members to generate a distinctive environment and to carry out their own vision of schooling" (Raywid 1996, 30–33). For the SLC staff to make, implement, and be responsible for decisions that meet the needs of their students, they must have sufficient autonomy and independence from the larger school. Because the comprehensive school principal typically remains responsible for the entire student body in a school with SLCs, power in the school remains centrally located in the site administration, along with the authority over teacher hiring, curriculum, course approval, budget, and master schedule—crucial elements of school operations that the SLC needs to control. In this environment, the successful implementation of the small design, the satisfaction of its teachers, and the likelihood of increased student outcomes are less certain. When the decisions of the SLC conflict with the interests of the large school, it is seldom that the large school makes accommodations. Instead, the SLC's success becomes dependent on the larger school's commitment and ability to honor the SLC's structure and its decisions. Tensions can emerge between the SLC and the whole school, and when there are multiple SLCs within a school, the SLCs may end up competing with each other to earn the favor of the principal.

The challenge of the SLC to maintain all the elements of smallness is not usually due to malevolence of a power-hungry building principal. If the large school attempts to institute a few elements of smallness while simultaneously committing to the large-school design, the large school's entrenched systems, its values of efficiency and specialization, and its bureaucratic tendencies will often overpower smallness, even if there is no specific intent to do so. Peter continues:

> What we've seen [when large schools implement discrete elements of smallness] is a strong pull back towards the more diffuse comprehensive high school, back towards routines that veteran teachers have been in where "I shut my door, and I do my own thing," back towards people thinking about their territory as adults in a building and not about student outcomes or collaboration. It's not easy to do any of this work, but it's really not easy to have one foot in both camps. The tendency is to slide

back to the comprehensive high school because it's easier. It's easier. The standards are lower in a comprehensive high school, where you're not being asked to do as much as a teacher and you're not being asked to do as much as a student.

Peter describes how the century-old identity of teachers and the culture of the large comprehensive high school will overpower discrete elements of smallness. As long as the SLC remains subject to the large school's decisions and vision, the energy and ideas of those teachers may be constrained, and the full merits of smallness won't be realized.

Deborah Meier makes this point more bluntly, believing that the implementation of smallness in anything less than a fully autonomous separate school will be frustrating and futile:

> It doesn't do us much good to know each other well if we can't use that knowledge. Nor do adults modeling good discourse serve much point if the discourse is only about the details, not ever about the big picture. Loyalties aren't engendered in schools that can't protect their own, that are controlled by rules that view adults and children as so many interchangeable parts. . . .
>
> A small school must be a school—not a school-within-a-school (whatever that is) or a "mini-school" or a house or a family. It can be just one of many housed in a shared building, but a building does not equal a school. A school must be independent, with all that the word implies, with control over a sufficient number of parameters that count—budget, staffing, scheduling, and the specifics of curriculum and assessment, just to mention a few. (Meier 1995, 115)

Following Meier's urging, some large schools have been redesigned into separate autonomous small schools within the larger campus, each with a different focus, mirroring the design of separate small colleges that comprise a larger university. In New York City and Chicago this work has been done on a large scale, but as one might expect, this arrangement is a delicate one. The principals of the campus schools must work with each other to share facilities and negotiate lunch schedules. More significantly, schools occupying the same campus, and often the same building, must mediate their different and sometimes conflicting cultures. In the best arrangements, however, small schools that co-occupy a larger building or campus can benefit by learning from each other and exchanging best practices to improve the quality of education in each of them.

Small schools can be created out of a large school either through a gradual transformation—in which the small schools grow and the large school is phased out— or through a radical restructuring, in which a large school is closed for a year, students are dispersed to neighborhood schools during the small-school planning, and the new small schools enroll the returning students the following year. Each of these strategies has its challenges: when the change is gradual, the old and new incompatible cultures occupy the same facility; when the change is all at once, the experience is more intense and often wrenching. And in some cases, small schools are created entirely from scratch, without any preexisting high school students, staff, or culture.

Which of these models of small-high-school development is most effective? The Gates Foundation recently evaluated its financial support of small schools and found that the percentages of small schools with achievement test scores above district averages were greater among new small schools than among those small schools that had been redesigned out of a larger school (National Evaluation of High School Transformation 2006). This suggests that small high schools carved out of an existing large school have the additional burden of the previous school's culture, staff, and history, which makes their success that much more difficult compared with new small schools, even if they occupy a former comprehensive school building.

Despite research supporting the educational merits of small high schools, the method of small-high-school development is often a result of political and financial considerations, as well as an assessment of practitioners' capacities and willingness to change. The deep feelings around changing the comprehensive high school, the resource investment inherent in structural reform, and the political concerns of superintendents and school boards impede the kind of radical change Meier advocates. SLCs within a comprehensive school therefore may be the result of a political compromise, not a deliberate decision about what is best for students.

The charter high school may be the most innovative model of small schools, freed from many of the rules and regulations that apply to other public schools in exchange for greater accountability for their students' results. Aside from following a few state laws regarding compulsory education and graduation requirements, all decisions about the school—from how money is spent to the daily schedule to the hiring and support of staff—are made at the school level. In exchange for this control, the school is held to its goals for student achievement and can be closed if it does not meet those goals. Given this opportunity to design a school with maximum autonomy and responsibility to best serve its students and staff, it should by now be no coincidence that charter high schools are rarely, if ever, large.

CONCLUSION

The question of identity—how we define ourselves as a school—is often an issue for small schools, and when teachers in comprehensive schools consider adopting elements of smallness, they face the same questions: what do we stand for, what are we willing to sacrifice, what experiences do we want to provide our students and teachers, and how do we build structures and systems to support them? The identity challenges for small schools are about how to become more enduring and resilient—how do we withstand changing circumstances and people to ensure reliability and constancy? Large schools that consider incorporating smallness have the opposite concerns: how able and committed are we to change a system that, although neither effectively serving significant groups of students nor providing meaningful opportunities for teacher collaboration, has been a fixture of our community for decades?

Because the evidence supports the benefits of small schools for students and teachers, the orientation of the solutions should be clear: the more integrity and protection of smallness, and the more autonomy, responsibility, and support for practitioners within that smallness, the more opportunity for improved student achievement. But still, most high schools remain large or adopt limited aspects of smallness that ask teachers to impractically "have one foot in both camps" of largeness and smallness. In the Conclusion, we'll review what we've learned so far, and we'll consider the following questions: how urgent is it that schools become small, and how assured can we be that they will be successful?

DISCUSSION QUESTIONS

1. How can we as educators make sense of the potential trade-offs when moving from a large school that serves many to a small school that serves fewer students more effectively? What arguments could be made in favor of such a move, or against it?

2. For whom might working in a small school be challenging, even not a good fit? How, if at all, might challenges and issues be handled? Which, if any, might seem insurmountable?

3. How might the kind and quality of work in a small school affect teachers with differing levels of experience—and therefore different developmental needs? How, if at all, might individual teachers' needs be met? Which, if any, might seem unable to be met, given the unique opportunities and constraints present in small schools?

FURTHER READING

Esquith, Rafe. 2007. *Teach Like Your Hair's on Fire: The Methods and Madness Inside Room 56*. New York: Viking.

Goodlad, John I. 1984. *A Place Called School: Prospects for the Future*. A Study of Schooling in the United States. New York: McGraw-Hill.

"Is Small Beautiful? The Promise and Problems of Small School Reform." 2005. Special issue, *Rethinking Schools* 19, 4.

Meier, Deborah. 1995. *The Power of Their Ideas: Lessons for America from a Small School in Harlem*. Boston, MA: Beacon Press.

CONCLUSION

WE KNOW FROM BOTH research and practitioner experiences that small high schools provide benefits to students that large comprehensive high schools cannot. The key elements of teachers' experiences that are possible in small schools but often absent in large schools include:

- personalized relationships between teachers and students, both within classrooms and school-wide;
- personalized relationships among teachers and staff;
- clusters of teachers who serve the same set of students;
- collaboration among adults that creates coherence across classes, grades, and the entire school;
- shared responsibility, mutual accountability, and collective ownership for the success of the entire school;
- teachers' voices having meaningful impact on schoolwide decisions.

Research clearly shows that when practitioners take full advantage of these opportunities, coupled with sufficient autonomy and authority, there are significant benefits, including:

- lower dropout rates
- fewer disciplinary infractions
- higher attendance
- higher graduation rates
- higher student achievement
- parent satisfaction
- teacher satisfaction and lower turnover
- greater sense of belonging among students and adults
- higher extracurricular participation rates
- differentiated learning experiences

In short, small schools can be so much more effective than large schools because having fewer students creates conditions that allow for powerful approaches to teaching and learning—conditions that are usually prohibited in schools with large numbers of students.

For example, we know that relationships and collaboration among adults in a school can affect what happens in classrooms. Unfortunately, these opportunities are limited, if they exist at all, in large schools. Teachers do not share students, they have little time to talk with each other or develop relationships with each other, and the sheer number of teachers makes consensus difficult. In a small school in which teachers are able to have intentional relationships and purposeful conversations with students and with each other, as well as expand their role and perspective beyond their own classrooms, they not only can affect teaching and learning experiences in each classroom, but they can also influence the school environment as a whole: its tone, culture, policies, and procedures; its mission and long-term direction; and the quality of teaching and learning that every member of the school experiences.

We've also seen how the organizational structure of schools changes what and how teachers think about the students and themselves. It's as if the systems of large and small schools allow, and may even require, certain beliefs, priorities, and behaviors from the staff, regardless of their individual beliefs and priorities. Michael Soguero suggests that despite the intent and beliefs of individuals within school organizations, large schools and their staffs must prioritize efficiencies:

> People work differently when they're in a small school. Somehow, when . . . people are overwhelmed by managing large numbers, it seems that managing the masses is the main concern. . . . In the small school you don't have to face the problem of moving thousands of students through the building. There's some tipping point . . . when you have enough students and there's enough distance and enough anonymity that the concerns . . . become about how to get them through the door in the morning, how to get them to lunch, how to feed them, how to get them from one class to another. . . . Just the sheer numbers alone make a tipping point into bureaucratic thinking versus thinking about teaching and learning.

The working conditions and organizational structures of large schools can have an enormous impact on teachers' experiences regardless of their beliefs. We have seen how some uniquely motivated and visionary teachers in large schools have implemented aspects of smallness that act against the depersonalizing systems. Yet, what takes significant initiative and perseverance in a large school–knowing students as individuals and establishing collegial relationships–can be an expectation and structurally supported in a small school.

We have also seen that simply reducing the number of students in a high school does not, by itself, create higher student outcomes. Small schools can simply replicate the systems, beliefs, and behaviors of large schools to become "miniature large schools," or what Michelle Fine calls "large schools in drag" (2005, 11). After all, a small school can ignore the opportunities of having fewer students and teachers, simply replicating a large school's impersonal isolation and bureaucratic hierarchy; it's certainly easier to "scale down" a familiar model of secondary education than to create something new. If the small school's staff does build relationships but stops short of using the relationships to focus on the rigorous work of high-quality teaching and learning, the students and staff may be happier than in a large school, but the staff will have failed in their responsibility to demand excellence from their students. If the principal remains the only decision-maker for schoolwide issues, and teachers don't have formalized collaborations, instruction will remain unchanged, and teachers will remain isolated and responsible simply "for delivering content lessons to students passing by on a conveyor belt" (Darling-Hammond 1997, 165). Small-school staffs must be focused and intentional about their work.

An example of this phenomenon is cited in the 2006 multiyear study of Chicago's initiative to redesign large schools into small schools, in which the researchers found that "although working in a small school did appear to encourage a greater sense of teacher collegiality, trust, collective responsibility, and related contextual features that might enable instructional reform activity, we did not see evidence that these contexts fostered more of the practices thought to facilitate instructional reform" (Kahne et al. 2008, 34). In other words, the small schools gave staff the chance to construct a stronger, more meaningful and effective educational program, but many of the small schools may have rested on their relationships or created the relationship-centered conditions of student and teacher work for their own sake. The only purpose of all the opportunities that small schools offer is to improve student achievement. If that is not the result, then what is the point of fewer students and better relationships?

Some might argue that even if the small school did nothing but construct relationships between teenagers and adults that made students feel safe and valued, it would be enough; those characteristics are generally absent from large high schools, where student anonymity jeopardizes school safety and impedes learning. But relationships aren't enough—not even close. Hugs aren't calculus, and although being known and valued is a vital prerequisite for learning, it is not the same as learning.

Moreover, in the midst of national rhetoric about the achievement gap in schools, we can't settle for underserved students just being better known in their schools (although it is certainly a step forward from where we are now). This is especially true because we know that when small schools take full advantage of their opportunities, they improve academic achievement specifically among low-income students and students of color. While it is well-known that there is a strong correlation between a student's socioeconomic status and her academic achievement, research over several years has shown that the larger the school, the stronger the correlation between socioeconomic status and achievement, and the smaller the school, the weaker the correlation. In other words, small schools have been shown to have an "equity effect" that weakens the bond between socioeconomic status and student achievement (Howley and Bickel 1999, 2000). Research in several different states has found that

Cross-Reference For more on the racial and ethnic dimensions of achievement gaps, see Book 4, Chapter 3.

> as schools become larger, the negative effect of poverty on student achievement increases. The less affluent the community served, the smaller a school should be to maximize the school's performance. . . . This well documented correlation between poverty and low achievement is much stronger—*as much as ten times stronger*—in the larger schools than in the smaller schools [in the study's

four states]. . . . While children of all races are as likely to
be affected by the relationship between school size,
poverty, and achievement, minority children are often enrolled in schools that are too big to achieve top performance in the community. (Howley and Bickel 2000, 10)

The researchers also found that in the states studied,
there were significant numbers of schools that, were they
smaller, would be more effective with their populations.
For example, in Ohio, 90 percent of the schools "are too
big to maximize achievement, given the income level of
the communities they serve, and would likely produce
higher scores if they were smaller" (Howley and Bickel
2000, 6).

The implications of these findings are enormous.
With this information available to us, we should structure our high schools to be small so that we can make in-
roads into reducing the achievement gap—a seemingly
intractable problem in our country. The only thing holding us, and our students, back is our political will. Why,
then, do there remain any large high schools?

One complication referenced several times in this book
is our intense cultural affection for our comprehensive
high schools, fueled by our "collective nostalgia," that invests them with particular inviolate attributes. As Deborah Meier writes, "The big, mindless high school, no
matter how dysfunctional, has many fans, including kids.
When we talk with school officials and local politicians
about restructuring large high schools, the first thing they
worry about is what will happen to the basketball or base-
ball teams, the after-school program, and other
sideshows; that the heart of the school, its capacity to educate, is missing, seems almost beside the point" (Meier
1995, 31–32). The large comprehensive school has been a
fixture in communities both physically and psychologi-
cally, having hosted years of sports contests, dances, grad-
uations, and, most important, memories for the adults in
the community who were enrolled in the school or at-

tended its events. The memory is likely rosier than the reality, which may have included years of dropouts and student failures, weary teachers, safety concerns, and frustrations with hard work that has led to incomplete successes. Peter Ross comments,

> [The large high school] is a tradition; it's a cultural institution in many places. There are many places in the country where the comprehensive school is the one thing that everybody in the community has in common, and you're going to break that up? "Why? We were state champions. I went there, and my parents went there." Or the kids who need the change the most are the most disenfranchised. The upper echelons of the community are still being served quite well by these comprehensive high schools. . . . They're still getting their AP classes and their honors track, and they're doing just fine. As Linda Darling-Hammond says, they don't need a small school; they already have one. Although I would argue that having been to a school like that myself, I could have used a lot more personalization than I got.

Consider that students in honors tracks usually have all the same classes with each other and share the same teachers. Within that structure, the teachers and students are actually enjoying the benefits of smallness, while those outside those specialized programs remain excluded from those relationships and personalization. Yet the benefits of smallness should not be reserved for only certain groups of students or be denied to students whose voices may be less influential.

Unfortunately, the reluctance to change the large high school is not just about sentimentality but also about protecting certain interests. Because small schools have been shown to have an "equity effect," reducing the correlation between socioeconomic status and student achievement, while large schools increase this correlation, it is reasonable that high-income families have less incentive to change a design that is working for them and to create small schools, for this could potentially deny them certain advantages they currently enjoy in large schools. In other words, if the dynamics and designs of large schools allow higher-income students and families to capitalize on their economic status, then their self-interest would drive them to resist small schools, where the advantages of their income have less impact. Perhaps this partly explains why most of the willingness to restructure large high schools is in communities that are predominantly low-income; there are fewer high-income people whose interests need to be considered.

Nevertheless, the benefits of small schools are now being recognized as benefiting all students, not just those in low-income schools (although families who have enrolled their children in small private schools have known this all along). Suburban and more diverse communities are beginning to restructure their comprehensive high schools and experience the advantages of smallness for students and their teachers. In West Clermont, a suburban district outside of Cincinnati, the large schools have been restructured into smaller schools. In addition, small high schools have been endorsed by the National Association of Secondary School Principals. Vermont, Maryland, and Florida have laws that either encourage schools to be smaller or mandate a maximum student body for them.

Another possible explanation for why small high schools are not more common is that elements of the large high school may be preferred by some adults who work there. Large high schools can offer more stability, more independent autonomy and privacy for teachers in their classrooms, and more specialized staffing. Instructional materials and policies are more established, and pedagogy is traditional. Teachers in large schools don't need to venture outside of their classrooms, don't need to expend the additional energy to be part of the larger school community, can focus entirely on their own classrooms, and don't need to know students as well. It is simply safer, with less pressure to change or innovate their practices.

Despite the research on what small high schools can create for students' and teachers' experiences, the political burden still remains on the small schools to prove that they, unequivocally, are best for students, while large high schools face no such scrutiny. Michelle Fine writes that small schools are "considered an experiment, while large schools are here to stay. When students fail in small schools, the schools are blamed. But when students fail in large schools, it is seen as the fault of the students!" (Fine 2000, 174). Perhaps it is time for the burden of proving educational effectiveness to shift from the small school to the large comprehensive school. As Goodlad writes in *A Place Called School*, "The burden of proof, it appears to me, is on large size. Indeed, I would not want to face the challenge of justifying a senior, let alone junior, high of more than 500 to 600 students (unless I were willing to place arguments for a strong football team ahead of arguments for a good school, which I am not)" (1984, 310).

In the Introduction I cited the sobering statistic that only 71 percent of our students graduate from high school. This statistic, in and of itself, should spur us to rethink our current public school system, in which most students attend large comprehensive high schools. But we are failing our students not only because of the high number of dropouts. Only about one-third of students who enter public high schools both earn a diploma *and* complete the necessary coursework to meet college entry requirements. The rates by ethnic group break down as follows: only 23 percent of African American students and 20 percent of Latino students, compared with 40 percent for white students—and even this number is unacceptably low (Greene and Winters 2005). Until we judge our comprehensive high schools on their educational effectiveness with preparing every student for postsecondary options, instead of their variety of programs and the scale of their activities, small schools will remain a novelty in our secondary public school landscape.

WHO WORKS IN SMALL SCHOOLS?

Teachers who are considering work in small schools, or who are exploring how they might implement smallness in their large school, should analyze how well the opportunities and challenges of smallness align with their beliefs about teaching and learning as well as their professional and personal goals.

> HEATHER CRISTOL: Some people are going to be right for [teaching in a small school], and some people would really prefer a larger, more conventional arrangement. The important thing is understanding who you are and what you're looking for. I've seen people come here [to teach at my small school] and just really not like it, and they could be perfectly happy somewhere else, at a different kind of school. There is a certain mentality, a certain set of skills, a certain set of interests that would make sense for a small school.

> STACIE PIERPOINT: It's not a piece of cake. Your hours tend to be longer because you are more visible and you are held more accountable. The small schools tend to attract the kind of person that is going to want to work and go that extra mile to make sure the kids are doing well. I think it is important to know that it is a lot of work. . . . The benefit is that you hopefully are going to see your students doing better in school.

> LARAVIAN BATTLE: You're going to work more in a small school than you would in a big school, but the benefit is that it should feel like a small community where everybody knows everybody . . . and your colleagues are much more likely to help you out when you

need it. You're more likely to help a friend than to help a stranger—that's just human nature.

So what kind of teacher is right for a small school? Beyond the appeal of small schools in the ways we've seen in this book, there seems to be an attraction of small schools to teachers who have certain beliefs about the larger social and political purposes of public education. It has been my experience that those who choose to work in small schools share some general beliefs about the conditions required for effective learning environments— conditions that may be possible only in small schools—and are driven to teach in order to address issues of equity, opportunity, and democracy. Not coincidentally, many small schools are poised to facilitate these same goals.

> STACY SPECTOR: [Traditionally in schools] I think there haven't been honest conversation about the beliefs adults have about student learning . . . to look at the achievement gap not only between students based on race, gender, ethnicity, and class, but the gap between where they are as learners and what they need to know and be able to do as learners. It comes down to the beliefs and values about learning, and it is about issues of equity and social justice that we engage in the work of small schools, not only on behalf of our students but with our students.

With all of their challenges, across the different and varied small schools, there seem to be some common beliefs:

> HEATHER CRISTOL: There's a prevailing liberal/ community organizer/political spirit to the small schools—this feeling that we're working with underprivileged kids, mostly poor, and we have an interest in exploring power and society. Our school mission is "understanding yourself, the world, and how to make

change," and there are a lot of small schools in New York that have some kind of focus around making change in society . . . so that's something that is a fit for some people and not for others.

Small schools, with their less hierarchical management structure, shared decision-making, and lack of tracking, can exemplify virtues of equity and democracy that are unfortunately absent in many large schools. If public high schools are expected to equip every teenager, regardless of income, ethnicity, or background, with the skills necessary to participate meaningfully as an American citizen, and to have an equal opportunity to succeed in the global economy, then small schools seem to show evidence that they are the most likely school structure to meet that expectation.

In their simplicity, small schools reveal what could be and what is not, that quality outcomes could be achieved by all, and that systemic equity requires high standards and innovation rather than standardization. Small schools strive to create justice in a society in which poor and working-class students so often are denied. . . . Small schools may be spawned by visionaries. But even more impressive, small schools create visionaries among educators and our young, who now believe that "what could be" must be, and what is, needn't be—that they can and must strive to promote social change in the public sphere within public schools. (Fine 2000, 174–175)

Teachers in small schools aren't there simply because they want fewer students; they are there because they believe that all students should be successful, and the way they believe they can maximize this possibility is to have fewer of them in their school.

In this book I have tried to capture what we know about how the number of students a school serves can have a major impact on the experience of its teachers.

The large school builds systems and structures to maximize efficiencies; the small school's systems are to facilitate personalized relationships. The small school is more susceptible to disruptions and mistakes than the large school, more easily led astray by competing interests within or outside it. What holds the small school together, through its challenges and threats, is the shared vision of its members, their accountability to each other, the greater purposes that guide their work, and the relationships that engender trust and courage among the students and their teachers.

When schoolteachers were considered interchangeable parts in a school system, the idea of teachers and schools being "a good fit" with a school had little meaning. Now that schools come in multiple sizes and are encouraged to have unique missions, programs, and cultures, it has become more important that every teacher work in the school that best matches her beliefs about education, schools, kids, and teaching and learning. Therefore, teachers should affirmatively *choose* the school in which they teach to the extent they can. And we all should—regardless of where we teach—aspire to help create a system of public high schools that can truly meet each student's needs. The information in this book, when viewed through the lens of your experiences, education, and your own larger purposes, may help you to make the right choice about where to work and what to advocate for.

So this book is less about small high schools than about powerful school practices and the ways that smallness facilitates them. The teacher who works in a small high school—one that uses relationships to develop personalized learning environments and a culture of joint work—experiences being a teacher differently than in a large high school environment. With smallness, teachers don't just teach without bells—a symbol of the impersonal and bureaucratic regulation of teacher practice—but teach without isolation in their classroom, without depersonalization of colleagues and students, and without regimented, factory-model efficiencies. These environmental features may have been acceptable, even preferable, when we expected less of many of our students and, perhaps, each other. If we want public high schools where every one of our students is successful, teachers need purposeful collaboration, mutual support, intentional relationships with our students to know them well, and voice. We know that these conditions are unavailable in most large comprehensive high schools, and while they may not be guaranteed in small-high-school environments, at least there the powerful practices we want, and our students deserve, are possible.

RESOURCE A:
TRACKING AND INEQUALITY

Research Findings

I N *KEEPING TRACK: How Schools Structure Inequality* (1985), her seminal work on tracking, Jeannie Oakes analyzed research on thirty-eight schools, of which twelve were high schools. The schools were of varying size, were located in different parts of the country, and served a range of student populations. What she found was that tracking, in one form or another, existed at every school and, more importantly, the experience of students in different tracks was significantly different. Ultimately, different tracks were exposing students to widely different educational experiences that seemed to reinforce and contribute to the separation and stratification of students from different ethnic, racial, economic, and social backgrounds. The following are some key findings of her research:

- In multiracial schools, students of color were found in disproportionately small percentages in high-track classes and in disproportionately large percentages in low-track classes (67).
- Much of the curricular content of low-track classes was such that it would be likely to lock students into that track level because the content that was omitted from that class was necessary for successful mobility to other tracks (78). In addition, the content omitted from low-track classes could essentially deny those students access to the full range of educational futures (91).

- The instructional environments of high-track classes were more characterized by a whole set of teacher behaviors thought to promote learning than were those of low-track classes (110). For example, teachers in high-track classes made instruction "understandable" by being clearer about what was to be learned (110). By contrast, behavioral goals for low-track classes were more closely linked to control than they were to learning (91).
- High-track students far more often agreed that their classmates liked one another and were willing to extend help. Classes in the lowest tracks were considerably more hostile and unfriendly places (127).
- Students in high-track classes had significantly more positive attitudes about themselves and had higher educational aspirations than did students in low-track classes (143).

Oakes's findings have been supported in subsequent research. For example, Gamoran (1987) found, based on a national survey that followed more than 20,000 students in grades 10–12, that students in academic tracks gained significantly more on tests of math, science, reading, vocabulary, writing, and civics than did students in the general and vocational tracks. In a startling finding, Gamoran showed that achievement gaps between students in different tracks were greater than the overall disparity between students who dropped out of school after tenth grade and those who stayed in school (150). Gamoran, Nystrand, Berends, and LePore (1995) found that aspects of quality instruction were unequally distributed in different class tracks, "magnifying achievement inequality [as] it contributes to overall achievement inequality among social groups" (709).

Teachers concerned with the effects of tracking are faced with two choices. They can work to eliminate tracking or strive to implement it more effectively. Eliminating tracking will raise the ire of families who perceive that heterogeneous classes will mean sacrificing opportunities (which will be true when teachers have not been trained in differentiation strategies that challenge every student) and for whom higher academic tracks have always translated into educational opportunities that other students have been denied. To choose this option is to take a stance that it is unethical and anathema to the purpose of public education that students sorted into higher tracks enjoy advantages at the de facto expense of students in lower tracks.

Alternatively, teachers and administrators seeking to address the inequities of tracking can take the more pragmatic approach and find ways to improve the structure and practices of tracking. First, they can explore ways that the tracking placements can be more flexible, either by reassessing students' abilities periodically to ensure accurate placement or by providing additional academic supports for students in lower tracks that enable them to "catch up"—to overcome the lack of skills and content knowledge that prevents them from moving out of the lower track. Second, they can find ways that teachers of low-track classes can be as skilled as teachers in higher tracks in offering high-quality instructional experiences (with professional development or by rotating teachers through different assignments) and ways that teachers can maintain high expectations for all students, regardless of track placement.

RESOURCE B: THREE WAYS SCHOOLS USE SCHEDULING TO REDUCE STUDENT LOAD

BLOCK SCHEDULING

Teachers see students for an extended time, but less often. Instead of the traditional schedule of a five-period week and a one-hour period for each class, a sample block schedule has classes meeting half as often but for double the length of time.

> Benefits: Smaller student load each day (except for Friday in this example); extended time for class activities

> Challenges: Less continuity, which may be more important for particular subjects (e.g., foreign language); when students are absent, they miss double the instruction

	M	T	W	R	F
Period 1	English	Social Studies	English	Social Studies	English
Period 2					Social Studies
Period 3	Math	Science	Math	Science	Math
Period 4					Science
Period 5	Phys Ed	Foreign Language	Phys Ed	Foreign Language	Phys Ed
Period 6					Foreign Language

INTENSIVE SEMESTER-LONG CLASSES

Compress yearlong classes into a semester, meeting for double the time each day.

> Benefits: Similar to benefits of block scheduling, with more intensive work throughout a semester; smaller student load

> Challenges: Similar to challenges of block scheduling—a semester-length break between sequenced courses that may depend and build on prior course knowledge (e.g., math, foreign language)

	Semester 1 (M–F)	Semester 2 (M–F)
Period 1	English	Social Studies
Period 2		
Period 3	Math	Science
Period 4		
Period 5	Phys Ed	Foreign Language
Period 6		

COMBINED COURSES

Two subjects are integrated and taught by a single teacher.

> Benefits: Smaller student load throughout entire year; opportunities to draw connections between related subjects

> Challenges: Teachers must be certified in multiple subjects; requires the teacher to have deep content knowledge in both subjects to meaningfully integrate

	M–F (entire year)
Period 1	English / Social Studies
Period 2	
Period 3	Math / Science
Period 4	
Period 5	Phys Ed
Period 6	Foreign Language

RESOURCE C: ADVISORIES

MANY SMALL SCHOOLS create structures to facilitate adult-student relationships in addition to, and sometimes in lieu of, creating smaller class sizes and smaller student loads. One common example is an "advisory" class, in which every adult is assigned a small group of students to be their counselor, advocate, and school liaison for the students' families. The advisories meet periodically (daily in some schools, less frequently in others) and provide a setting for relationship-building through group activities and conversations. Advisory content can vary, ranging from academic content and skills (sex education, test-taking strategies, study skills, literacy and math support, postsecondary planning) to social skills (handling peer pressure, managing responsibilities, and resolving conflict). Advisories can be constructed across grades or within a single grade, but students generally remain with the same advisor for multiple years to maintain a long-term relationship with the adult and to build a tighter sense of community among their fellow advisees.

The implementation of advisories can be more challenging than many schools anticipate. Some teachers are natural counselors for students, but others have difficulty facilitating interactions among and with students distinct from how they manage their classroom. Advisory programs also require a high level of investment in planning and teacher training. When an advisory is implemented without sufficient support and preparation, it can devolve into a homeroom-type period in which time and conversations are unstructured. When an advisory is considered to be an additional class, with goals and expectations for both students and teachers, it can be part of a powerful support system for students. Some large schools have tried to institute advisories to facilitate the kind of relationships found in small schools, but it is often difficult to do so successfully because advisories require additional training and resources, must be integrated into a large inflexible master schedule, and as an additional course to teach and plan may run afoul of teacher contracts. By contrast, in small schools, advisories are adopted more naturally because the organization is designed to facilitate the kinds of relationships that advisories support.

RESOURCE D: A PROTOCOL FOR LOOKING AT STUDENT WORK

ONE TOOL SCHOOLS use to share and discuss a teacher's practice is to examine student work—a specific work product of an assignment. To formalize and guide the teachers' conversations with each other about student work, and to ensure structured safety for the discussion, schools use protocols. Below is a protocol adapted from one created by the National School Reform Faculty (http://www.nsrfharmony.org): "Atlas: Learning from Student Work Protocol." Atlas Learning Communities is a comprehensive school improvement model founded in 1992 by James Comer, Howard Gardner, Theodore Sizer, and Janet Whitla.

I. GETTING STARTED

- The facilitator reminds the group of the norms: no fault [the purpose is to build capacities of teachers, not to indict them for their weaknesses], collaboration [we work together to solve problems], and consensus [each person's opinion counts] and, with the group, establishes time limits for each part of the process.

Note: Each of the next four steps should be about 10 minutes in length. The presenter is silent until "Reflecting on the Discussion," step 5. The group should avoid talking to the presenter during steps 2–4. It is some-times helpful for the presenter to pull away from the table and take notes.

- The educator providing the student work gives a very brief statement of the assignment. The educator should describe only what the student was asked to do and avoid explaining what he or she hoped or expected to see.
- The educator providing the work should not give any back-ground information about the student or the student's work. In particular, the educator should avoid any statements about whether this is a strong or weak student or whether this is a particularly good or poor piece of work from this student.

Note: After the group becomes more familiar with this process for look-ing at student work, you may find it useful to hear the educator's expecta-tions. However, this information will focus more of the group's attention on the design of the assignment, the instruction, and the assessment, rather than on seeing what is actually present in the student's work.

2. DESCRIBING THE STUDENT WORK

- The facilitator asks: "What do you see?"
- During this period the group gathers as much information as possible from the student work.
- Group members describe what they see in the student's work, avoiding judgments about quality or interpretations about what the student was doing. [In other words, at this stage the participants focus strictly on what they observe in the student work itself, rather than make interpretations about the stu-dent's thinking or the teacher's instructional strategies— elements the group addresses in subsequent questions.]
- If judgments or interpretations do arise, the facilitator should ask the person to describe the evidence on which they are based.
- It may be useful to list the group's observations on chart pa-per. If participants offer interpretations about the work in-stead of focusing only on observations, they can be listed in another column for later discussion during step 3.

3. INTERPRETING THE STUDENT WORK

- The facilitator asks: "From the student's perspective, what is the student working on?"
- During this period, the group tries to make sense of what the student was doing and why. The group should try to find as many different interpretations as possible and evaluate them against the kind and quality of evidence.
- From the evidence gathered in the preceding section, try to infer what the student was thinking and why; what the student does and does not understand; what the student was most interested in; how the student interpreted the assignment.
- Think broadly and creatively. Assume that the work, no matter how confusing, makes sense to the student; your job is to see what the student sees.
- As you listen to each other's interpretations, ask questions that help you better understand each other's perspectives.

4. IMPLICATIONS FOR CLASSROOM PRACTICE

- The facilitator asks: "What are the implications of this work for teaching and assessment?"
- Based on the group's observations and interpretations, discuss any implications this work might have for teaching and assessment in the classroom. In particular, consider the following questions:
  - What steps could the teacher take next with this student?
  - What teaching strategies might be most effective?
  - What else would you like to see in the student's work?
  - What kinds of assignments or assessments could provide this information?
  - What does this conversation make you think about in terms of your own practice? About teaching and learning in general?

5. REFLECTING ON THE DISCUSSION

- The presenter shares what they learned about the student, the work, and what they're now thinking. The discussion then opens to the larger group to discuss what was learned about the student, about colleagues, and about themselves.

6. DEBRIEFING THE PROCESS

- How well did the process work—what went well, and what could be improved? If the group has designated someone to observe the conversation, this person should report his or her observations.

For additional student work protocols, see the Coalition of Essential Schools' website: http://www.essentialschools.org/cs/resources.

REFERENCES

Alliance for Excellent Education. 2009. *The High Cost of High School Dropouts: What the Nation Pays for Inadequate High Schools.* Washington, DC. August.

Ayers, William, Gerald Bracey, and Greg Smith. 2000. *The Ultimate Education Reform? Make Schools Smaller.* Milwaukee: Center for Education Research, Analysis, and Innovation, University of Wisconsin–Milwaukee.

Banks, James, ed. 2004. *Handbook of Research on Multicultural Education.* 2nd edition. San Francisco: Jossey-Bass.

Barker, Roger G., and Paul V. Gump. 1964. *Big School, Small School: High School Size and Student Behavior.* Stanford, CA: Stanford University Press.

Blanchard, Alan P., and Brooke Harms. 2006. *Transforming the High School Experience: The Practitioner's Guide to Small Learning Communities.* Victoria, BC: Trafford Publishing.

Broughman, Stephen P., Nancy L. Swaim, and Patrick W. Keaton. 2009. "Characteristics of Private Schools in the United States: Results from the 2007–08 Private School Universe Survey." Table 7. Washington, DC: National Center for Education Statistics.

Campbell, R. J. 1985. *Developing the Primary Curriculum.* London: Holt, Rinehart and Winston.

Center for Collaborative Education. 2006. "Progress and Promise: A Report on the Boston Pilot Schools." Boston, MA.

Clinedinst, Melissa. 2008. *State of College Admission 2008.* Edited by David A. Hawkins. Arlington, VA: National Association for College Admission Counseling.

Coalition of Essential Schools (CES). 2006. "The CES Common Principles: Elementary and Secondary School Inclusive." CES National Web. http://www.essentialschools.org/pub/ces_docs/about/phil/10cps/10cps.html.

Coladarci, Theodore, and Casey D. Cobb. 1996. "Extracurricular Participation, School Size, and Achievement and Self-Esteem among High School Students: A National Look." *Journal of Research in Rural Education* 12, 2: 92–103.

Cotton, Kathleen. 1996. "School Size, School Climate, and Student Performance." School Improvement Research Series. Close-Up #20. Portland, OR: Northwest Regional Educational Laboratory.

———. 2001. "New Small Learning Communities: Findings from Recent Literature." Portland, OR: Northwest Regional Educational Laboratory.

Crosnoe, Robert, Monica Kirkpatrick Johnson, and Glen H. Elder, Jr. 2004. "School Size and the Interpersonal Side of Education: An Examination of Race/Ethnicity and Organizational Context." *Social Science Quarterly* 85, 5: 1259–1274.

Darling-Hammond, Linda. 1997. *The Right to Learn: A Blueprint for Creating Schools That Work.* Jossey-Bass Education Series. San Francisco: Jossey-Bass.

Dewey, John. 1956. *The School and Society; The Child and the Curriculum.* Chicago: University of Chicago Press.

Editorial Projects in Education. 2007. *Diplomas Count 2007: Ready for What? Preparing Students for College, Careers, and Life after High School.* Bethesda, MD: *Education Week.*

———. 2008. *Diplomas Count 2008: School to College: Can State P-16 Councils Ease the Transition?* Bethesda, MD: Education Week.

Fine, Michelle. 2000. "A Small Price to Pay for Justice." In William Ayers, Michael Klonsky, and Gabrielle Lyon, eds., *A Simple Justice: The Challenge of Small Schools*, 168–179. The Teaching for Social Justice Series. New York: Teachers College Press.

———. 2005. "Not in Our Name: Reclaiming the Democratic Vision of Small School Reform." *Rethinking Schools* 19, 4: 11–14.

Fitzsimmons, William R. 1991. "Risky Business." *Harvard Magazine* 93 (January–February): 23–29.

Fowler, William J., Jr. 1995. "School Size and Student Outcomes." In Benjamin H. Levin, William Fowler, and Herbert J. Walberg, eds., *Advances in Educational Productivity*, vol. 5. Greenwich, CT: Jai Press.

———, and Herbert J. Walberg. 1991. "School Size, Characteristics, and Outcomes." *Educational Evaluation and Policy Analysis* 13, 2 (Summer): 189–202.

French, Dan, Mary Atkinson, and Leah Rugen. 2007. *Creating Small Schools: A Handbook for Raising Equity and Achievement.* Thousand Oaks, CA: Corwin Press; Boston: Center for Collaborative Education.

Gamoran, Adam. 1987. "The Stratification of High School Learning Opportunities." *Sociology of Education* 60, 3: 135–155.

Gamoran, Adam, Martin Nystrand, Mark Berends, and Paul C. LePore. 1995. "An Organizational Analysis of the Effects of Ability Grouping." *American Educational Research Journal* 32, 4: 687–715.

Gay, Geneva. 2000. *Culturally Responsive Teaching: Theory, Research, and Practice.* Multicultural Education Series. New York: Teachers College Press.

Gladden, Robert. 1998. "The Small School Movement: A Review of the Literature." In Michelle Fine and Janis I. Somerville, eds., *Small Schools, Big Imaginations: A Creative Look at Urban Public Schools*, 113–133. Chicago: Cross City Campaign for Urban School Reform.

Goodlad, John I. 1984. *A Place Called School: Prospects for the Future.* A Study of Schooling in the United States. New York: McGraw-Hill.

Greene, Jay P., and Marcus A. Winters. 2005. "Public High School Graduation and College-Readiness Rates: 1991–2002." New York: Manhattan Institute for Policy Research.

Hammersly, Marvin. 1984. "Staffroom News." In Andy Hargreaves and Peter Woods, eds., *Classrooms & Staffrooms: The Sociology of Teachers & Teaching.* Milton Keynes, UK: Open University Press.

Hargreaves, Andy. 1994. *Changing Teachers, Changing Times: Teachers' Work and Culture in the Postmodern Age.* London: Cassell.

Howley, Craig B. 1994. "The Academic Effectiveness of Small-Scale Schooling (An Update)." ERIC Digest 372 897. Charleston, WV: Clearinghouse on Rural Education and Small Schools.

———. 2002. "Small Schools." In Alex Molner, ed., *School Reform Proposals: The Research Evidence*, 49–77. Greenwich, CT: Information Age Publishing.

Howley, Craig B., and Robert Bickel. 1999. "The Matthew Project: National Report." Randolph, VT: Rural Challenge Policy Program.

———. 2000. "When It Comes to Schooling . . . Small Works: School Size, Poverty, and Student Achievement." ERIC Digest 447 973. Randolph, VT: Rural School and Community Trust.

Howley, Craig B., and Aimee A. Howley. 2004. "School Size and the Influence of Socioeconomic Status on Student Achievement: Confronting the Threat of Size Bias in National Data Sets." *Education Policy Analysis Archives* 12, 52.

Kahne, Joseph E., Susan E. Sporte, Marisa de la Torre, and John Q. Easton. 2008. "Small High Schools on a Larger Scale: The Impact of School Conversions in Chicago." *Educational Evaluation and Policy Analysis* 30, 3: 281–315.

Ladson-Billings, Gloria. 1994. *The Dreamkeepers: Successful Teaching for African-American Students.* San Francisco: Jossey-Bass.

Lee, Jihyun, Wendy S. Grigg, and Patricia L. Donahue. 2007. "The Nation's Report Card: Reading 2007." NCES 2007-496. National Center on Education Statistics.

Lee, Valerie E. 2004. "Effects of High-School Size on Student Outcomes: Response to Howley and Howley." *Education Policy Analysis Archives* 12, 53: 1–15.

Lee, Valerie E., and Julia B. Smith. 1995. "Effects of High School Restructuring and Size on Early Gains in Achievement and Engagement." *Sociology of Education* 68, 4: 241–270.

———. 1997. "High School Size: Which Works Best, and for Whom?" *Educational Evaluation and Policy Analysis* 19: 205–227.

Leithwood, Kenneth, and Doris Jantzi. 2009. "A Review of Empirical Evidence about School Size Effects: A Policy Perspective." *Review of Educational Research* 79, 1: 464–490.

Levine, Eliot. 2002. *One Kid at a Time: Big Lessons from a Small School.* The Series on School Reform. New York: Teachers College Press.

Lieberman, Ann. 1995. "Practices That Support Teacher Development: Transforming Conceptions of Professional Learning." *Phi Delta Kappan* 76, 8: 591–596.

Little, Judith Warren. 1990. "The Persistence of Privacy: Autonomy and Initiative in Teachers' Professional Relations." *Teachers College Record* 91, 4: 509–536.

———. 2002. "Professional Community and the Problem of High School Reform." *International Journal of Educational Research* 37, 8: 693–714.

Lortie, Dan C. 1975. *Schoolteacher: A Sociological Study.* Chicago: University of Chicago Press.

McGuire, Kent. 1989. "School Size: The Continuing Controversy." *Education and Urban Society* 21, 2: 164–174.

Meier, Deborah. 1995. *The Power of Their Ideas: Lessons for America from a Small School in Harlem.* Boston: Beacon Press.

Mohr, Nancy. 2000. "Small Schools Are Not Miniature Large Schools: Potential Pitfalls and Implications for Leadership." In William Ayers, Michael Klonsky, and Gabrielle Lyon, eds., *A Simple Justice: The Challenge of Small Schools,* 139–158. The Teaching for Social Justice Series. New York: Teachers College Press.

Monk, David H. 1987. "Secondary School Enrollment and Curricular Comprehensiveness." *Economics of Education Review* 6, 2: 137–150.

Monk, David H., and Emil J. Haller. 1993. "Predictors of High School Academic Course Offerings: The Role of School Size." *American Educational Research Journal* 30, 1: 3–21.

National Association of Secondary School Principals. 1996. *Breaking Ranks: Changing an American Institution: A Report of the National Association of Secondary School Principals in Partnership with the Carnegie Foundation for the Advancement of Teaching on the High School of the 21st Century.* Reston, VA: National Association of Secondary School Principals.

National Center for Education Statistics (NCES). 2007. *Digest of Education Statistics.* Table 92. Washington, DC: National Center for Educational Statistics.

———. 2008. *Digest of Education Statistics.* Tables 3, 5, 87. Washington, DC: National Center for Educational Statistics.

The National Evaluation of High School Transformation. 2006. "Evaluation of the Bill & Melinda Gates Foundation's High School Grants Initiative: 2001–2005, Final Report." Washington, DC: American Institutes for Research; Menlo Park, CA: SRI International.

Oakes, Jeannie. 1985. *Keeping Track: How Schools Structure Inequality.* New Haven, CT: Yale University Press.

Obama, Barack. 2009. "Remarks of President Barack Obama—as Prepared for Delivery: Address to Joint Session of Congress, Tuesday, February 24, 2009." http://www.whitehouse.gov/the_press_office/remarks-of-president-barack-obama-address-to-joint-session-of-congress/.

Powell, Arthur G., Eleanor Farrar, and David K. Cohen. 1985. *The Shopping Mall High School: Winners and Losers in the Educational Marketplace.* Boston: Houghton Mifflin.

Raywid, Mary Anne. 1985. "Family Choice Arrangements in Public Schools: A Review of the Literature." *Review of Educational Research* 55, 4: 435–467.

———. 1996. "Taking Stock: The Movement to Create Mini-Schools, Schools-Within-Schools, and Separate Small Schools." Urban Diversity Series No. 108; ERIC Digest 396 045. New York: ERIC Clearinghouse on Urban Education; Teachers College, Columbia University.

———. 1999. "Current Literature on Small Schools." ERIC Digest 425 049. Charleston, WV: ERIC Clearinghouse on Rural Education and Small Schools.

Rouse, C. E. 2005. "Labor Market Consequences of an Inadequate Education." Paper prepared for the Symposium on the Social Costs of Inadequate Education, Teachers College, Columbia University. October.

Sapon-Shevin, Mara. 1994. *Playing Favorites: Gifted Education and the Disruption of Community.* Albany: State University of New York.

Schiefele, Ulrich. 1991. "Interest, Learning, and Motivation." *Educational Psychologist* 26, 3: 299–323.

Schiefele, Ulrich, and Mihaly Csikszentmihalyi. 1994. "Interest and the Quality of Experience in Classrooms." *European Journal of Psychology of Education* 9, 3: 251–270.

———. 1995. "Motivation and Ability as Factors in Mathematics Experience and Achievement." *Journal for Research in Mathematics Education* 26, 2: 163–181.

Sizer, Theodore R. 1984. *Horace's Compromise: The Dilemma of the American High School: The First Report from a Study of High Schools.* Boston: Houghton Mifflin.

"Small Learning Communities." 2002. National Conference on State Legislatures.

Swanson, Christopher B. 2009. *Cities in Crisis: Closing the Graduation Gap: Educational and Economic Conditions in America's Largest Cities.* Bethesda, MD: Editorial Projects in Education, Inc.

Toch, Thomas. 2003. *High Schools on a Human Scale: How Small Schools Can Transform American Education.* Boston: Beacon Press.

Tomlinson, Carol Ann. 1999. *The Differentiated Classroom: Responding to the Needs of All Learners.* Alexandria, VA: Association for Supervision and Curriculum Development.

Tomlinson, Carol Ann, and Cindy A. Strickland. 2005. *Differentiation in Practice: A Resource Guide for Differentiating Curriculum, Grades 9–12.* Alexandria, VA: Association for Supervision and Curriculum Development.

Tyack, David B. 1974. *The One Best System: A History of American Urban Education.* Cambridge, MA: Harvard University Press.

Tyack, David B., and Larry Cuban. 1995. *Tinkering toward Utopia: A Century of Public School Reform.* Cambridge, MA: Harvard University Press.

Vygotsky, L. S. 1978. *Mind in Society: The Development of Higher Psychological Processes.* Edited by Michael Cole et al. Cambridge, MA: Harvard University Press.

Wagner, Tony. 2001. "Leadership for Learning: An Action Theory of School Change." *Phi Delta Kappan* 82: 278–383.

Walberg, Herbert J., and Herbert J. Walberg III. 1994. "Losing Local Control." *Educational Researcher* 23, 5: 19–26.

Wasley, Patricia, Michelle Fine, Robert Matt Gladden, Nicole Holland, Sherry King, Esther Mosak, and Linda Powell. 2000. *Small Schools, Great Strides: A Study of New Small Schools in Chicago.* New York: Bank Street College of Education.

Interviews

- Josh Anderson, former Kansas Teacher of the Year, correspondence, June 11, 2009
- LaRavian Battle, small-school algebra teacher, Oakland, California, phone conversations, April 20, 2009, and July 20, 2009

- Mary Beth Blegen, 1996 National Teacher of the Year, correspondence, June 5, 2009
- Paul Cain, large-school math teacher and former Texas Teacher of the Year, phone conversation, June 20, 2009
- Heather Cristol, small-school English teacher, Brooklyn, New York, phone conversation, April 23, 2009
- Steve Gardiner, former Montana Teacher of the Year, email correspondence, June 19, 2009
- Avilee Goodwin, small-school dance teacher, Oakland, California, phone conversation, April 16, 2009
- Brian Greenberg, small-school English teacher and former large-school teacher, Los Angeles, California, phone conversation, June 6, 2009
- Stacie Pierpoint, small-school Spanish teacher, Washington, DC, phone conversations, April 1, 2009, and July 14, 2009
- Peter Ross, director of LEADS (Leadership, Equity & Accountability in Schools and Districts) Network at Stanford University, Stanford, California, phone conversation, April 6, 2009, email correspondence, June 3, 2009
- Alan Sitomer, former California Teacher of the Year, phone conversation, June 12, 2009
- Michael Soguero, small-school principal, Estes Park, Colorado, phone conversation, April 28, 2009
- Stacy Spector, former small-school teacher and principal, Citrus Heights, California, phone conversation, May 4, 2009
- Barbara Yeatman, small-school curriculum facilitator, Humble, Texas, phone conversation, May 4, 2009

INDEX

ABOUT THE AUTHOR

Joey Feldman is Director of Secondary Education in Union City, California. In his nearly twenty years in public education, Joey has assisted with the oversight, development, and support of dozens of small schools. He has been a principal of a school-within-a-school and principal of two small charter schools, one of which he helped to establish. He has worked in the New York City Department of Education's Office of New Schools, and was a Fellow in the U.S. Department of Education's Office of the Secretary.

Prior to his work with small schools, Joey was a high school English and history teacher in Georgia. He has a BA in Humanities from Stanford University, an EdM in Teaching and Learning from Harvard, and a law degree from New York University. He lives in Oakland, California.

He is the author of "Still Separate, Still Unequal: The Limits of Milliken II's Monetary Compensation to Segregated Schools," in *Dismantling Desegregation: The Quiet Reversal of Brown v. Board of Education* (with S. Eaton and E. Kirby) and "Standing and Delivering on Title VII's Promises: White Employees' Ability to Sue Employers for Discrimination Against Nonwhites," in the *Journal for Law and Social Change*.